Space Music

by Jack Meehan

Space Music

Edited by John Meehan
Cover art by Tim Meehan
Back cover photo by Ashley Meehan
Design by Erik J Skinner

ISBN-13: 978-0615492407
ISBN-10:   0615492401

For my wonderful wife Edithe Angela

Contents

Part Two - Blue Devils

Part Three - Transitions

Acknowledgments

I would like to thank Patti Whaley for her time, perseverance, and commitment to making me more aware of the English language as a communication device. I would also like to thank my wife Edie and sons John and Tim for all of their help in putting this creation together and for the memories they shared.

Part One

Beginnings

Chapter 1
1950-1966 Kingsmen, Skyliners, USAF

I was eight years old when I first heard the sound of an outdoor brass ensemble. It was during a small neighborhood parade in the north Bronx: the consecration of a local Catholic Church.

My mom was holding my hand as I slipped between a few people to see what was making all the wonderful sounds I was hearing. As I stepped through the crowd, off the curb, and into the street, I found myself only inches away from the marching members of the Kingsmen Drum and Bugle Corps as they paraded by, playing loud and clear the sound that would live in my dreams for the next 45 years.

I can still recall vividly the blue satin blouses, bright red cummerbunds and big brass bells. I was transfixed! For that moment in time I existed all alone in a world of sound. The glorious sound of brass.

It took me two years to convince my mom and dad that I was serious about wanting to be a part of what I had experienced. I wanted to join the corps. And luckily, the William E. Irwin American Legion Post, which was where the Kingsmen rehearsed, was only three short blocks away from our apartment house on Kingsbridge Avenue, in the Bronx.

And so, in the winter of 1952, at the tender age of 10 I was off to join up with drum corps.

My very first memory of learning to play a horn was an experience I will never forget. There were three of us, just beginning, and we were situated up a narrow, creaky old set of stairs that brought us to something like a choir loft. I can still recall the smell of the place, nothing terrible, just very interesting and complex. There was musty and dusty, mixed with the smell of brass and beer. And to make it even more interesting, the older gentleman who instructed us in the art of spitting a

piece of string from the tip of our tongues, smoked a rather potent smell-
ing cigar… all the time! He would get right up in your face and show
you how he spit the string off his tongue. It was pretty intense for a 10
year old I'll tell you.

One year later I was in the hornline playing third soprano and learning how to march.

My fondest memory of those wonderful years was having soprano
sectionals downstairs at the corps hall. There was a two-lane, manual
bowling alley downstairs and if you wanted to bowl somebody had to
be the pin boy.

The pin boy was the guy who got to pick the bowling ball up after
someone had thrown it as hard as possible at the pins, send it back to
the bowler, pull the dead wood from the alley, and jump out of the way
before being bonked with a heavy bowling ball or pin.

If you played your parts correctly during sectional rehearsal, you got
to bowl, if you played them incorrectly, you got to be the pin boy.

I did not want to be the pin boy!

So I made sure I could play my parts perfectly… Just like Bobby
Kelly!

Bobby Kelly was my first real live idol. He could double tongue and
triple tongue and play high notes with a pretty tone. And he knew all of
his music. And he was always there at the end of practice, standing out
on the front steps of the hall with a joke and a hearty laugh.

By the time I was 12 years old I could double tongue and triple
tongue and play high notes with a pretty tone.

* * *

I remember being in Washington D.C. for the American Legion National Championship in 1954. A few moments of the trip are clear and
strong in my memory.

In those days the left goal line of the competition field was the starting line. All drum corps had to enter the field of competition over that
starting line.

A few yards behind the starting line was the inspection line, which
was where every individual in each corps was looked over by the in-

specting judge for personal neatness as well as condition and cleanliness of uniform and equipment.

A few yards behind the inspection line was the ready line, where the members and staff of the next corps to move up to the inspection line were preparing to be inspected.

So, what I recall so vividly from the 1954 national competition in Washington D.C. was standing on the ready line with people walking by, picking little pieces of lint, string, or what have you from me as though I were a toy soldier being spiffed up for display.

I recall a five second glimpse of standing perfectly still in the hot sun on the inspection line waiting for the man to come in front of me so I could present both myself and my horn to his keen inspection.

From that point on I have no memory of the starting line or of performing the show. My next recollection is of having my neck roughly scrubbed at the end of the show by one of the moms who had a towel soaked with witch hazel. It was like being brought back to life, all of a sudden, with no memory of what had just occurred. Did I really march the show? I guess I did because I remember having sweated up a storm.

My final drum corps memory from our nationals trip occurred the night of the senior corps final show. We sat way, way up at the top of the stadium, and it seemed like I was looking at the competition field through the wrong end of a pair of binoculars.

It was very exciting! I had never seen anything like it.

But my flash of memory was of the Geneva Appleknockers and their wonderful soloist Frankie Farr. I still don't quite understand what it was that happened that night but it was as if Frankie and the Appleknockers were able to captivate the attention of the audience.

The audience was mesmerized!

Frankie and the Appleknockers held the crowd in the palm of their hand.

This made a huge impression on me. I loved the idea of leading an audience into a state of rapt concentration.

* * *

In 1955 the Kingsmen hired George Rodriquez to be our new horn instructor. George played louder, higher and hotter than anyone I had ever heard. He was a "Latin from Manhattan." He liked to have fun as much as he loved to play his horn.

George was our instructor for the years of 1955 and 1956. He would come to rehearsal, teach us a new tune, then walk around in back of the lead line and play these juicy obbligato parts that would just knock my socks off.

Since no one had yet taught me to read music I would try to hold the musical image of what he had played in my head, so I could practice it mentally on the way home, and when I got home, and when I went to bed, and first thing in the morning... if I could remember it.

One Saturday, at the completion of a late afternoon marching rehearsal in the Kingsbridge Armory, I asked my brother Bill if we could stay and listen to the Skyliner hornline rehearse. The Skyliners were a senior drum corps and George Rodriquez was one of the soloists. Actually, George would switch with Bill Hayes. One would be in the Caballeros and one would be in the Skyliners. Bill Hayes was the celebrated instructor for the Blessed Sacrament Golden Knights.

At any rate, as we walked back into the armory, which was absolutely cavernous with all manner of army vehicles parked around the perimeter, I heard, for the first time and forever, a mature brass ensemble playing alone, without percussion. They were playing *I Only Have Eyes For You*, and it echoed around the armory in a dreamy kind of way, as if it came from everywhere at once. I was in heaven. I can still hear that sound inside my head any time I wish. It is indelibly imprinted there. Hard wired in.

* * *

It was during the year of 1956 that the Kingsmen disbanded, stranding a group of the neighborhood kids and myself; leaving us without a place to play and improve.

I dealt with my drum corps famine by gorging myself on drum corps recordings such as Liberty Bell '52 or Reilly Raiders '55 or St Joe's of Newark '54. I knew every solo on every record. I used to go up on the roof of our six-story apartment house and practice the music I had heard on the recordings, that was until the lady who lived on the sixth floor would come out onto her fire escape and shout foreign obscenities at me. Then I would just practice the fingerings.

We heard about a drum corps over in the east Bronx, the Sam Young Post. It was just a parade corps but beggars can't be choosers. So we all piled into one of those old checker cabs that could hold about seven people (Johnny Guarino, Richie Woods, Bernie Weeks, Eddie Gallagher, Ritchie Wunder and yours truly) and headed into the east Bronx.

As fate would have it luck smiled down upon us.

Shortly after we joined the Sam Young Post there was a merger between our corps and the New York Skyliners and I was suddenly the happiest guy in the world.

Hy Drietzer, a living legend in east coast drum corps, would be our instructor.

I was surrounded at every rehearsal by a fine group of players.

One in particular was Tommy Martin, soloist extraordinaire, my newest idol. Tommy could double tongue, triple tongue and play notes higher than any I had ever heard, with a sweet tone, and louder than a police siren.

This was definitely what the doctor ordered. Every rehearsal was an exciting event to be looked forward to and prepared for. Somehow deep inside me I knew that this was my chance and I had better not blow it. No pun intended.

* * *

It was 1957; I was 15 years of age and attending Cardinal Hayes High School in the Bronx, just a few blocks from Yankee Stadium. I had one favorite class in high school and that was jazz band.

I still had problems reading music but if you played it for me once, I could play it right back, and usually better. The best part of being in the jazz band was that they sometimes let me play the Harry James solos; my favorite being *Man With A Horn*; a slow, sweet, sexy tune which proved to be a real boon for getting dates after school dances.

Jazz band was great but school was a bummer, it just wasn't my thing. As a matter of fact, except for the year I spent in fourth grade with teacher Sister Gabriel, who I had hoped to someday marry, I disliked spending my time at school.

We stand up straight when we're young
Before we're sent for schooling
Before we're sat down in a chair and told
"There's just no time for fooling"
That's when I first became aware of boredom in my body
That's when I began to think of going to the potty
Anything to just get up and let my body wander
Let my mind investigate see, touch, feel and ponder!
I was trapped inside a desk that didn't really fit me
Hoping that the teacher didn't get upset and hit me
It's just not right to disconnect a kid's mind from his senses
To keep him from the world at large alone with no defenses
So I propose that children be the center of their learnings
So they can learn to know themselves and understand their yearnings
So they can learn some self control both physical and mental
And spend their lives contentedly exploring what they find
S p e c i a l

* * *

For three great years in the Skyliners I was privileged to stand next to such wonderful players as Tommy Martin, Bucky Swan, Ernie Fessler, George Rodriquez, Johnny Guarino, Joe de Figlia, Pepe Nataro and so many more. They were all players. Out of nowhere one of them would just pick up his horn and perform for you. If I had a problem figuring out how a part went, all I had to do was ask, "Hey, can anyone play this part?" and one of them would pick up his horn and give me his hottest rendition right then and there. And as you recall, I only had to hear it once.

The person who commanded my utmost attention was the corps' arranger, Hy Drietzer. Hy knew exactly what he wanted to hear musically and would use any means available to help the performers bring his music to life. He was intense, he was joyous, he exuded tremendous amounts of energy to get us to understand and perform nuance and subtleties others would fail to even notice. Hy was a genius and a wonderful man, and he arranged music that was heartfelt, exciting and completely New York.

At age 18 I left the Skyliners, went to work for the Burroughs Corporation in New York, and just kind of hung around drum corps for a few years.

During the summer of 1962 I was seriously considering going into the service. Tommy Martin and a few other good friends advised that I should think about trying out for the Air Force Drum and Bugle Corps stationed at Bolling Air Force Base in Washington, D.C. They said it would be good for me, and that I would meet some really fine people. Tommy had been in the Air Force Corps for the last three and a half years and said, "Hey Jacky, go ahead and try out, what could you lose?"

So since Tommy Martin was one of my special idols, I decided that what was good enough for Tommy was good enough for me.

* * *

Enter Truman Crawford and the marvelous Air Force Drum and Bugle Corps. This was an experience not to be missed. I found myself surrounded by the most intense, insane, creative, and talented people you could ever imagine.

Tru Crawford, in my humble opinion, was the most professional arranger in the drum corps activity. His music was clear, precise, and true to the original harmonies and character of the music he arranged.

Indeed, Tru Crawford had a multi-faceted personality. It seemed he would approach a situation from a sufficient number of viewpoints to see it clearly, make a choice using clarity and efficiency as his rule, and proceed to handle the situation in an intelligent, humane, and many times humorous manner. I thought Tru Crawford was a terrific human being. He added to my life over the many years I knew him, and I thank God I was in the right place at the right time to have experienced his particular charm and musical grace.

To tell the truth, I don't remember spending a lot of time rehearsing in the Air Force Drum Corps. Pretty much it seemed that all we had to do was play through a piece of music once or twice and that was it. It was really quite amazing. Everyone knew what they were doing! They could all read music!

Unheard of!

Even I understood music notation well enough by that time to decipher the arrangements we were given.

The really great thing about being in the Air Force Corps was getting to know and enjoy the wide range of personalities that went together to create the best sounding drum corps in the world.

My number one choice of all around best buddy was Ray Eyler. Ray Eyler is still, in my mind, the nicest person I have ever met. He introduced me to his wonderful family. He played duets from the Amsden duet book with me so as to help speed along my reading prowess. Both he and his brother filled my head with great sounding champion barbershop quartet and chorus recordings. And, Ray took me to a rehearsal of the Archer-Epler Musketeers of Upper Darby, Pennsylvania, which began a wonderful friendship with a terrific group of guys.

Ray Eyler was honest, sincere, and more talented than anyone deserves to be. I will never forget Ray and how he enriched my life.

By far the most professional sounding of all the brass players in the Air Force Corps was John Simpson. John's tone quality, pitch control and musicianship were astounding. He made his baritone horn sing. The sound was alive and vibrant. It may have only been a G-D bugle but in his hands it was the finest of musical instruments.

To finish out this trio of idols I would like to say a word about our go-to guy, our fearless leader, the man whose rehearsals were more fun than functional, Sergeant Ricardo A. Gabriel, known to all as "Gabe." Gabe took care of me and kept me out of trouble, which I was wont to get into. He taught me that it was possible to turn on the classical music station in his new Ford Galaxy and say immediately what was playing and who wrote it. I found this totally amazing and endeavored from then on to learn as much as I could about classical music.

I was only in the Air Force for nineteen months before they decided to disband the corps and give everyone the opportunity to change career fields, relocate to the Air Force Academy Drum and Bugle Corps in Colorado Springs, or separate out of the Air Force all together. I informed the man behind the desk very distinctly that I wanted "OUT." I loved the experience but found that I was not really cut out for military life.

* * *

For the next two years I worked for "Ma Bell" in the Bronx as a switchman. I studied trumpet with Carl Ruggiero, taught several small drum corps in Brooklyn and Queens, and fell asleep on my bed night after night all wrapped up with my trumpet and Arban's book.

I had no idea where I was headed but somehow the thought occurred to me that it would be best if I were at least well prepared for whatever was coming.

In 1966 the Casper Troopers came to town and played a show at Gaelic Park in the Bronx, only a few blocks from where we lived on Kingsbridge Avenue. The stands at the stadium were so close to the side line that it felt like you were right out on the field with the corps. That performance was an absolute thrill for everyone present. The Trooper mystique had struck and I was completely taken by the sheer power of their presence. So much so that I became aware of something deep inside me saying, "Go west young man."

I went to the VFW National Convention in Jersey City and took in a few Trooper rehearsals. I spoke to Greg Carr, a baritone player in the corps who seemed more than willing to tell me all the tall tales of Jim Jones and the Troopers. He brought me over to their equipment truck and displayed the painting of "F Troop" on the side, which he and others had rendered on canvas.

Just being around the Troopers felt wholesome, professional, and focused. Everyone seemed to know what was to be done and did it.

The Troopers went on to win the 1966 VFW Championship and it all became part of history, that is except as far as I was concerned. To me the Casper Troopers felt more like a piece of the future than a part of history.

Chapter 2
Tea Leaf Reader Predictions

In early September of 1966 Tommy Martin called and asked if I would like to accompany him on a trip across the country to visit a few of our mutual friends from the Air Force Corps. And while we were at it, he said he would like to go up to Wyoming and spend some time with Jim Jones and the Troopers. I said I would think about it.

When my good friend Johnny Guarino's sister Theresa heard about this possible trip, she said that we needed to go downtown right away to have my tealeaves read. It sounded strange but Theresa was very insistent.

The tealeaf reader told me I was going to take a trip out west and that I would meet my future wife and find good fortune. On the way down to the subway after the tealeaf session Theresa looked me straight in the eyes and said, "Jacky, I hate to say this but, you gotta go."

I called Tommy Martin the next day and told him I was ready to leave at any time. "When do we start?"

A few weeks later we left New York and headed west. I can still recall being energized by anticipation as we crossed over the George Washington Bridge in Tommy's new maroon Lemans and began our journey on highway 80.

We drove and talked and listened to the radio. I watched Tommy make faces as he drove, almost as if he were exercising the muscles around his mouth. I may not have mentioned it before but Tommy Martin had a tone quality that was sweet, pure, and extremely powerful throughout the full register of the instrument. So I started thinking that maybe his "face making" habits had something to do with his ability to control a very powerful air-stream. Needless to say, there were now two of us making faces throughout our long drives, but I believe I was the only one in the car who was aware of the fact.

We stopped in a tiny little town in Indiana to visit a few of Tommy's aunts. We were definitely down home in Indiana. In comparison to New York it was a little slow and dreamy. I learned how to make tortellini soup, and, I got to sleep in a real feather bed.

Next day we were back on the road driving, talking, listening to the radio and separately making faces at the windshield. We were headed for the home of John Simpson in "you guessed it" Kansas.

Our time with John was fun and reminiscent. We ended up talking about funny experiences with old girlfriends and eventually fell exhausted into bed. I thought it was odd that one could get so tired by just sitting in a car for ten hours, but that was the case.

A good night's sleep and we were back on the road again. My facial muscles felt like they were getting huge from all the exercise. I got the feeling that my mouth was turning into a fist.

We were headed due west and there was nothing but flat level ground all around us. Kansas is truly flat. Miles later we could just make out the Rocky Mountains in the distance. We were headed for the United States Air Force Academy in Colorado Springs and as we drove, and listened to the radio, and made our faces, the Rockies just kept getting bigger and bigger until it became obvious that we were definitely not in Kansas any more.

Nestled as it is in the lush green foothills of the Rocky Mountains, the United States Air Force Academy is both beautiful and enchanting. In Colorado Springs, Tommy and I spent some time walking through the Garden of the Gods, a large area filled with huge monolithic red rock forms, which somehow resemble living creatures.

We visited with Keith Markey, the musical director of the Air Force corps, and were completely blown away with his latest arrangement, *The Cincinnati Kid*, which was performed live for us by the brass section of the United States Air Force Academy Drum and Bugle Corps. That night we attended a party thrown by all of our old buddies from the Washington D.C. days. As might be expected, the party was a bit rowdy but lots of fun, with both old and new war stories being told.

I thought Colorado had a wonderful spirit about it, the vast scenic views, the clarity and lightness of the air all went together to create a feeling of renewal within my being. I felt at ease, completely and totally comfortable with the world.

As we drove north on interstate twenty-five I was thrilled to see signs pointing out places like Laramie and Cheyenne, Wyoming, and as we drew closer to Casper we saw signs pointing to the Goose Egg Ranch and Medicine Bow cutoff.

Wyoming was everything you might imagine the old west to be. After all those cowboy westerns I had seen on TV I found myself anticipating the Indians suddenly appearing over one of those far ridges.

Wyoming was rugged. Sagebrush, gullies, ravines, and huge snow-dusted red rock formations streamed past our windows. Believe it or not, we actually stopped at Independence Rock and took touristy pictures with my new thirty-five millimeter Canon camera purchased only the day before from a member of the Academy Drum Corps.

Casper was a town of about fifty thousand people, comfortably settled at the base of Casper Mountain's north slope at an altitude of about seven thousand feet above sea level. Casper seemed to be a nice quiet place.

Much different from New York City!

No roving gangs, no noisy subways. Casper was slow, safe, and hospitable.

Mr. Jones was immediately likable. He was both interesting and interested; he was sincere, industrious and multi-talented. He was an architect, a businessman, percussionist, state of the art drill designer, director, instructor, and he made one hell of a cheese omelet.

After introductions were over and pleasantries exchanged Mr. Jones asked me point blank, "So what are your plans for the future?"

To say the least I was surprised to have so much attention suddenly directed toward me. Jim Jones was a very intense individual. I had already mentioned to him about working for the New York Telephone Company, and that I would love to go to college but that it was not easy working full time and living in New York City. So I told him that I was concentrating on improving myself, developing my talents so I could be well prepared and at my best when my big opportunity came along.

That was when I told him about the tealeaf reader and what she had seen in my future. He found that most amusing and proceeded to explain how much he needed help with teaching the hornline during the winter months and on tour in the summer.

At that point Mr. Jim Jones made me an offer I couldn't refuse.

He said that if I were willing to move out to Casper he would pay me a stipend to teach the corps, secure a scholarship for me at the local junior college, find me a place to stay with a corps family and arrange for a transfer to the local phone company.

How do you like that? So far the tealeaf reader was batting a thousand. Now all I had to do was find my wife!

Before we left Casper for our long ride home, I told Mr. Jones that I needed time to sort everything out and that I would call and let him know my decision within a couple of weeks. Jim took a parting shot and said that if I did come out, he would supply me with a plane ticket to go home for a visit during the 1967 Christmas season.

Tommy and I left the land of the Troopers and headed back along the northern route, over the great lakes through Canada. By the time we arrived home I had a face full of muscles and a mind full of turmoil. How could I leave home, family, and friends, travel thousands of miles, with everything I own (AR speakers and turntable, Scott amplifier, LP collection, trumpet, bugle, clothes etc.) carefully packed away in my 1965 Sunbeam Alpine, and head courageously out into Indian country, alone, in the dead of winter?

Oh, by the way, my high range on the trumpet went up a fourth the first week back from the trip. Embouchure exercises do work!

Chapter 3
1967 Troopers - Casper College

I left New York on a cold, clear day in early January 1967. My little red Sunbeam was packed to the gills. The trip was quick and uneventful. The car ran well and the weather stayed basically cold and clear until I hit Douglas, Wyoming, just sixty miles from Casper.

It was close to midnight. The wind was blowing and the snow kept falling. I remember going through the center of Douglas and seeing the giant Jackalope statue in the middle of the street with snow falling all around it. Douglas looked like a ghost town with streetlights. I slipped out the other side of town and continued down the two-lane ribbon of black top that would take me to Casper and a good night's sleep.

Twenty miles outside of Douglas I hit a patch of ice and took a dive off the side of the road, down into a gulley about six feet from the shoulder. The car was still running but I was going nowhere. I shut the car down and got out to see what my situation looked like. It felt like the temperature was only in the twenties but the wind was blowing so hard that I found it hard to open the car door. The snow wasn't threatening but was consistent.

I walked down the road a bit to see if the car was visible. I could see the left rear light assembly, so I went back to the car and turned on the blinker lights. I recall thinking to myself that this could be the end of a beautiful beginning. "A fella could die out here!"

I decided to sit and wait a while to see what might happen. It wasn't long before I saw lights coming down the road from Douglas. I stood just to the side of the road and started waving my arms frantically. My luck was still holding out. It turned out to be a large eighteen wheeler with a winch on the front. The driver said I was lucky he came along, "there might not be another vehicle come this way for quite some time." He pulled my little red sports car out of the gulley quite carefully, and said I should follow him into Casper, and that's exactly what I did.

I found out the next day that the wind had been blowing at eighty miles an hour and that the wind chill was down in the single digits.

* * *

1967 was a year of high points and hard work. The expectations of a class A drum corps were new to me, as they were to many of the young Troopers in the hornline. It was a rebuilding year, which is not unusual after a winning season such as the Troopers had just experienced. There was much in the way of teaching and learning to be done if the corps was to be competitive in the coming year.

Every few months we were visited by Don Angelica who would arrive like a guardian angel bringing new arrangements, fun, laughter, and much needed inspiration. He accomplished more with the hornline in one rehearsal than I could in a month. He knew exactly what to say and how to phrase it to bring about a deeper sense of musicianship from the performers. When he spoke, the kids, the staff, and anyone else within hearing range listened. Don knew he was good at what he did and he flaunted it with a flamboyant personality. Don was great!

The staff had wonderful show meetings, which were always held at Mr. Jones' house. Mr. Jones, Don Angelica, Fred Sanford, Pete Emmons and whoever else may have been in town for the special rehearsals would be there. You could get a real sense of how the show would eventually come together by listening to the creative ideas being bounced around the room.

Show meetings at Mr. Jones' house were fun and creative!

I was learning something most intriguing at that time about my own personal awareness. When Don Angelica came to visit on his whirlwind weekends, he would usually ask me to warm the hornline up and direct them through a certain passage of music.

What I noticed from being placed in this situation was that when

Don was behind me, perhaps enjoying his morning cup of coffee, my awareness of the ensemble's playing was slightly different than usual. I somehow listened more critically to what was being played. I almost felt that I was hearing what Don might be listening for.

This I found to be a most important lesson. At any one moment there are many aspects of life happening at once and we have the ability to vary our perspective in order see and understand more clearly that which is before us.

Aha!

When Don Angelica would leave Casper and go back home to New Jersey, the hornline and I remained behind, practicing away in the NCHS band room, doing the best we could to get the music learned and memorized.

We had five or six good size practice rooms around the back of the band room and I found that when I sent the hornline into small groups (sections) they would work quite industriously. This left me free to take members out individually and supply them with information that would help them to grow and mature as brass players.

Taking the performers out individually also gave me the opportunity to get to know them better and at the same time evaluate their playing skills. I always had my horn with me so I could play parts along with them or show them little tricks, fun things like double tonguing, trilling, or jazz shakes. I wanted them to feel at ease with me and with their instrument.

Long weekends of all day drum corps were not easy. It was hard work and I had to get used to it. Rewarding, perhaps, but mentally draining.

The '67 repertoire of *Hallelujah Trail, Battle Hymn, Impossible Dream, Black Saddle, Bonanza* and *Promised Land* (from How the West Was Won) was chock full of things for me to deal with, not the least of which was learning how to read a full score. I had at long last become accustomed to reading my own individual part, but reading all the parts at once was a challenge beyond. I remember plodding through scores at night trying to figure out the baritone and alto rhythms, which were nothing like the rhythms one might find in a lead soprano part.

I found it necessary to keep all aspects of good ensemble playing fresh in my mind at all times. It was not a good idea to focus too strongly on one facet or another. I had much to learn about class A competitive drum corps. I had been given this opportunity and was determined to make good.

Jim Jones had made good on his end of our bargain too. I was set up with a great family of people who were all involved with the corps. Don Carr, the dad, could fix anything from a broken down bus to a busted bugle. His son Michael had just graduated from the corps and was off to college. Sons Gregg and Brett were both fine baritone players in the A corps, and Alice, the mom, helped out with sewing and various corps related projects.

I was enrolled at Casper College carrying eighteen units with a major in music, and working for the local phone company doing similar things as I had done in New York.

Corps was hard but life was wonderful.

So here I was taking a completely new look at life. My life in Casper felt like a vacation of sorts. Everything was new. Every experience was a brand new experience. You could say that life felt spontaneous: unpredictable in a word. Come to think of it, the weather was unpredictable too! I eventually discovered that eighty mile per hour winds, zero temperatures, dust storms, rain, snow, or golf ball size hail falling from the sky were not all that uncommon, especially on the back side of Casper College, which was set right up into the foothills of Casper Mountain.

It was very exposed indeed! The wind blew straight down the north side of the mountain and came crashing into the back of Casper College, right along the connecting walkway between buildings. Believe me, it got pretty wild sometimes. Have you ever been pelted by sleet coming at you at eighty miles per hour? Not a pretty sight!

I was extremely fortunate to have been thrust by fate into this situation where I could experience clarity: living free from the emotional bindings of past inhibitions. I had been given a chance to reinvent myself. I was free to become the me I might truly wish to be.

Once again, fate stepped in and directed my awareness to a wonderful philosophical life style; experience the world as always fresh and new, full of possibilities and spontaneity. Take what comes, deal with it the best you can, and move on.

There was no doubt about it. I was in the right place at the right time and I knew it.

As summer came on I realized that I had never given any thought to how the Troopers traveled around the country. Of course I knew it was by bus, but I could never have conceived the myriad possibilities of being stuck on a bus, all day, heading towards the next scheduled or unscheduled stop, perhaps to eat, or rehearse, or compete in a show, or more often than not just to go potty. Often enough we would find ourselves completely stopped, sitting along the side of a road, in the middle of nowhere, sometimes for hours, waiting for the buses to return from who knew where.

* * *

It was necessary for the Troopers to travel over a thousand miles just to get to where the competitions were held, and here we were, finally on our way down the road. It was the very first competition excursion of the year known as the evaluation swing.

Every year Mr. Jones brought the Troopers east to the midwest to get an early season evaluation of show design and performance qualities. Although the color guard was not judged as a separate caption, Mr. Jones expected to generate lots of general effect with the powerful and magnificent Casper Troopers' Color Guard.

The members of the Troopers were kept very well informed. Mr. Jones would sit for hours with them explaining the system by which they would be judged. He would talk to them about their personal responsibilities while performing, as well as the image they were to portray after performance. He would inform them of the way they were to handle themselves in the lunch line, or out in public. He would speak individually as well as generally to them about what he had observed of their practice technique during rehearsals, or he might take time to tell them about all the wonderful things one could do in New Orleans on free day. The Troopers were a family in every way and there was no doubt about it, Mr. Jones was (as he might put it) the benevolent dictator.

The 1967 evaluation swing was my first exposure to the judging community and I found them to be very helpful. The judges of the Central States Judging Association were willing to give critical insight as to the corps performance from both the technical point of view and that of the overall general effect.

In those days the technical aspect of the brass, percussion and marching captions was adjudicated by using the "tic" system, which meant that for every mistake the judge saw or heard he would put a tic in the proper column on the evaluation sheet. Sometimes the judge would write down a group of tics and put a circle around them, which meant that the cluster of errors all happened at the same place in the show. This was sometimes referred to as a unit penalty.

CSJA judges like Ed Morrissey and Earl Joyce were amazing. Their ability to recall where and when errors occurred during our show was uncanny. I mean these guys had some serious memory skills to be able to recall so much information about the tics recorded on the page. As you can tell, I was thoroughly impressed.

The act of adjudication in the area of technique (tic system) was said to be an objective form of evaluation whereas general effect adjudication was considered subjective. The general effect judge assigned points based on a "buildup" system. The drum corps was given credit for the effects generated by their show.

There was one brass technique judge in particular who seemed to adjudicate differently than all the other judges. His name was Bob Spevacek. Mr. Spevacek believed that all or at least most of the errors being committed by brass lines were tone and intonation based. So when you received Mr. Spevacek's evaluation, almost all of the tics would be of the tone and intonation variety, few attack or release errors, timing or balance errors, or cracks, only intonation errors. This seemed rather strange since the word "objective" means based on fact, not on personal opinion, but it was obvious that Mr. Spevacek's personal opinion was that tone and intonation were the backbone of solid musical performance.

So what I took away from this was that you didn't have to be a professional musician to play attacks, releases, and rhythmic figures together, but that it took a certain degree of "professionalism" to tune instruments in such a way as to play with a sense of unerring intonation. The idea was that tone quality and intonation basically separated the men from the boys as far as brass performance was concerned.

Once again my "Aha" light went on.

The Troopers survived the evaluation swing very well and went home to Casper to accompany Mr. Jones at his favorite pastime…

"Rehearse! Rehearse! Rehearse! If we get this right then Katie bar the door." You can bet that by the time we left on Nationals tour every suggestion of worth and every negative aspect of the corps' show would be addressed, rehearsed, spit polished, cleaned and clipped. Rumor had it that the Troopers practiced blindfolded but I can tell you for certain that they only did it with their eyes closed.

The corps typically rehearsed at the industrial building complex out on the west end of town, but at this time of year Casper was gearing up for the Central Wyoming Fair and Rodeo.

Yahoo!

So here I was, the boy from New York City who had never been to a fair, much less a rodeo, and I was totally jazzed, that is until I saw where the corps was going to perform.

The performance took place in the actual rodeo arena where horses, cows, and bulls romped and stomped, and where those same animals were presently trying to bust out of their holding chutes. It had rained earlier that day so the dirt, which wasn't all dirt, and the moisture that wasn't all from the rain, had coalesced into a lumpy, gooey, nightmare for a shiny pair of shoes. I could not believe that the reigning world champion Casper Troopers were actually going to put a show on in a giant wet cow patty, but they did. After the performance, which was really quite fun to behold, the corps looked like it needed to be hosed down and blow-dried.

The members changed clothes in the parking lot, the uniforms were sent to the only two dry cleaners in town, who apparently knew the drill, and the "kids" were given the rest of the day off to enjoy the festivities.

After a few more days of spit, polish, and practice the corps was ready and eager to get on the road. They loaded up the equipment truck and the three buses outside of Mr. Jones' house and proceeded to wait for Mr. Jones to finish the many odds and ends he had to deal with before he could take his place on the lead bus and give the tally-ho signal. New Orleans, here come the Troopers!

It was a very warm tour; just think Chicago, New York, and New Orleans in August. The air conditioning on the buses would come and go. Card games would be played. Fuel stops would provide time to get together with people from the other buses just to chat or get cooled down inside of the truck stop.

I became adept at finding shady, refreshing places for the hornline to warmup and rehearse. My thought was that I would do anything to help them feel at ease in the incredibly tense atmosphere that existed around this level of competitive drum corps.

My teaching style was very positive in nature. I believed in wholehearted individual performance and was slow to integrate the idea of squeaky clean, meaning, no audible faux pas, blunders, or slip-ups. I wanted to promote uniformity without sacrificing self-expression and without diminishing self-confidence. I wanted the line focusing on the idea of hot performance, not shying away from making mistakes. I discovered that what I wanted was to create an environment of mutual respect and trust where information was freely given and openly received.

And so we came to the high point of the nationals trip: Free day in New Orleans. The morning of free day was taken up with rehearsal. The national competition was only days away.

That morning after rehearsal I asked a lovely young lady by the name of Edie Booth if she would accompany me to see the sights of the city. Edie was in the colorguard. I had seen her at rehearsals but we had never had an opportunity to talk.

Edie seemed to hesitate when I asked. I thought to myself, she was probably thinking of all the reasons she shouldn't go out with a twenty five year old guy from New York City, but she finally smiled and said she would.

We strolled about the city in a leisurely way, talking and taking in the sights. It seemed that neither of us was in a hurry. We came to a small lake with paddleboats. The lake was lined on all sides with big old trees, and from the trees hung long strands of grey green moss like foliage. In the center of the lake was a small island upon which we landed and disembarked. It was here that I popped the question.

I asked Edie if she would ever consider leaving Casper if the opportunity presented itself.

Why I asked this question I am not quite sure, but Edie's answer was definite and for sure. She said "Oh no, no. I couldn't possibly leave Casper."

I proceeded to tell her about all the things I had experienced from jazz at Birdland, to Broadway shows, to motor biking around Bermuda, to warm nights on Miami Beach, and I told her that I really wanted to get to see California some day.

And so the day went, talking and walking, stopping to take pictures with my Canon thirty-five millimeter camera and tripod. Edie was easy to be with. She didn't seem to have any particular agenda like so many people have. There was no compulsive talking. We were just two people enjoying where we were and one another's company.

Late that afternoon, the buses picked the corps up and brought us all back to the motel to shower and change for the evening portion of free day. Mr. Jones thought it was very important for the corps to have a night out on the town, to experience what they might never have a chance to experience again. And besides, Mr. Jones loved good food and he told everyone which restaurants were best. Edie and I chose The Court of the Two Sisters at 613 Rue Royale in the French Quarter.

Edie looked beautiful. I had never seen her dressed up before and at only seventeen, she was a knockout. We both felt quite comfortable with the atmosphere of the French Quarter. It was still a bit warm out but pleasant, balmy I suppose you might say, with live music and the sounds of merriment coming from all directions. It wasn't bright or glitzy; it was subdued, slow and easy; very relaxed, and yet, stimulating in a down south, sultry kind of way.

Both the wonderful dinner at the Court of the Two Sisters and Edie's youthful companionship were a delight. The evening slipped pleasantly by and all too soon came to an enjoyable but raucous end; riding back on the bus with everyone boisterously telling of their free day adventures, all at the same time.

VFW Nationals came and went. The Troopers placed second, just four tenths of a point behind the Cavaliers. For me it was a year like no other. I learned so many new things about drum corps, about life, and about people that I felt I needed time to take it all in and digest it, because soon I would have to decide if this was the direction I wanted to take with my life.

Chapter 4
1967 Troopers Tour

I rode the bus back to Casper. It was a lot quieter on the way back than it had been on the way out. And now that the pressure of the season had subsided I was able to just sit quietly, allowing myself to assimilate the events of the last eight months. It had truly been a whirlwind of a ride. See the USA from the window of a Trooper bus.

When we finally reached Casper I went back to the Carrs' house, put the top down on my little red sports car, hopped in and set off for the top of Casper Mountain for some much needed solitude. I had a lot of thinking to do and I knew just the place to do it.

To get to the top of Casper Mountain I headed south toward the foothills, past the college and all of its out buildings, then up the slow grade that leads to the foot of the mountain.

The climb up the mountain offers switchbacks galore and great overlooks where one can view the whole of Casper, along with a hundred mile panorama of the wild west, laid out before you like a virtual map. On a super clear day the view seemed to go on forever. But it wasn't the overlook I had in mind. I was headed for my favorite place in the whole world, which lay just on the other side of the mountain.

The top of Casper Mountain is all dirt roads, and in the winter can be very slippery and dangerous but in late August the roads were hard and dry. I drove over the top of the mountain and rode down into the valley between green rolling hills. The weather was absolutely perfect. There was no wind and the temperature was about eighty degrees. I stopped the car and turned the engine off. Immediately I experienced a sensation of numbness about my entire head. It was as though I had gone completely deaf.

I heard not a sound, except for the ticking of the catalytic converter. I just sat there for a while and allowed my ears to adjust slowly to the extreme quiet. One by one I could distinguish individual sounds within the silence. I could hear insects buzzing far out in the meadow, and birds, far away in the trees, creating their gentle symphony of sounds. Nothing disturbed this place of solitude. It was here that I gained energy and felt at peace.

* * *

The fall semester of 1967 brought with it an added bonus. For the first time in my life I was turned on to reading books. Literature, the virtual world of paper and print where you can while away many happy hours without really doing anything.

The person responsible for this new attitude toward reading was my humanities teacher, Mr. Hanselman. He was a kindly professorial type in his late fifties or early sixties. He had a way of enticing you into wanting to know the rest of a story. He would begin a tale in class, and then, when he felt the interest of the class pique, he would assign the rest of the story for homework and move on to something new. He made learning interesting in a way that I had never experienced.

I recall one evening in particular. Mr. Hanselman invited the whole class over to his home for popcorn, a warm fire, and a wonderful recorded version of Don Quixote de la Mancha. The experience was tantalizing. Just the idea of losing oneself in a fantasy of fiction grabbed at my attention.

The experience took me back to memories in the Bronx, sitting on the floor at maybe five or six years old, listening to a 78 rpm recording of Robin Hood with Basil Rathbone as Robin.

Our phonograph at home was an old windup. It didn't run on electricity. It had no wires! You had to wind it up and keep it wound up or it would slow down and all the pitches would get slower and lower. The phonograph was inside of a large wooden cabinet and when the top was lifted you could see a picture of a little black and white dog listening intently to a "Victrola" phonograph player.

I loved listening to the stories but what I enjoyed most was the music. The music made the stories come alive. It could both stir and sooth the emotions. For instance, the musical score for Robin Hood was performed by a variety of heralding trumpets and horns, which were memorably combined with the strong male voices of Robin Hood's merry men. Our recording of Aladdin and His Wonderful Lamp featured the beautiful and enchanting music of Rimsky-Korsakov's Scheherazade.

When I was in high school I had been able to get B's without ever cracking a book. All I had to do was pay close attention in class. It wasn't that I couldn't read, it was just that I hadn't yet found a first-rate reason to apply myself to the task.

Mr. Hanselman was first-rate. Through his efforts I became a book lover. I would gobble up anything from King Arthur to Plato on Socrates. I loved Camus and Kafka. I became especially fond of folk tales like Beowulf and The Song of Roland. It was like I couldn't get enough. I was hooked.

* * *

When I wasn't reading, studying, practicing, going to school, working at the phone company, or teaching Trooper rehearsals, Edie and I went out to see the newest and hottest movies playing in downtown Casper. There were only two movie houses in Casper and they were right around the block from one another.

We were on our way to the Rialto Theatre to see the new art film Elvira Madigan. Edie said that her Uncle George owned a candy store – soda fountain – tobacco shop, on the corner of Second and Center Streets right next to the Rialto Theatre.

While we stood in line waiting to get our tickets for the movie, Edie proceeded to tell me all about the Greek side of her family. Edie was very animated. She told me that her Grandmother Panos "lives right upstairs in the apartment building just fifteen feet from where we're standing which, by the way, is also owned by my Uncle George, but my

Grandmother had once lived in a big beautiful yellow and white house situated prominently on the corner of Second and McKinley about ten blocks east of here."

It was fun being out with Edie. She seemed to have a little New Yorker in her attitude. She was straight forward, honest, bright, and beautiful. What more could a fella ask?

* * *

Don Carr and I worked together on a big project that fall. We were changing the Troopers' bugles from a G-D-F# to a G-F-F# configuration. The process involved cutting tubing, soldering, measuring, refitting, and testing. It was done in a cozy little shop located out in back of Don Carr's house.

I remember spending many wonderful hours back there with Don. He was truly a master when it came to anything mechanical. His mind was a monument to organization and method.

He was at ease while he worked.

He moved at a steady pace with ease and grace. And he taught me all about working with tools and torches, and about remaining patient, mindful, and neat. He taught by example and I learned quickly.

I was also becoming an amateur photographer, shooting a couple rolls of film a week. Mostly black and white, since the Carr family had graciously allowed me to set up a darkroom in the basement that I could use for developing and printing black and white film. I had never done anything like that before. I found it fascinating to be able to take an idea from its inception, develop it through varied steps, making judgments and decisions, leading ultimately to the final process and the finished product.

A complete creative process existed there at my fingertips. Whatever my "photo-op" mind could conceive, I could then bring to life on paper. I definitely went overboard on this project. I spent way too many hours enraptured in the darkroom.

* * *

As promised, Mr. Jones came through with a roundtrip ticket to New York for Christmas.

Going home for a visit was fun. It's always nice to be the center of attention for a while. Of course, everyone seemed the same, except for me. I felt at home, and yet I felt out of place. I felt as though someone had switched worlds on me, like I had entered a parallel universe. About midway through the holidays I began to relax. The immediacy of all things Casper faded and I was able to just be there, at home and at ease.

On the plane trip back to Trooperville I contemplated the changes that my perceptions had gone through during the holiday season. I thought to myself, "why am I not just me all the time? Why is my mind somewhere other than where my body is? Why did I experience my family and friends through an invisible filter of life in Casper?"

It seemed that, beyond my awareness, I had been involved in a whirlwind of Casperian thought, even though I was no longer physically in Casper. I vowed to sign up for the psychology 101 course in the spring semester to help figure out this mind-body ambiguity. The burning question was: Is there a part of me that remains stable and constant, totally aloof from the effects of the outside world?

It seems I was just beginning to explore the possibilities of present moment experience; that is to say, existing wholly within the present moment; clear of the mental confusion caused by reverberations of past experiences, which tend to cloud our perceptions of present reality.

This little tidbit of observational awareness was monumental in its effect on my future endeavors.

Chapter 5
1968 Troopers - Fred Sanford

The Natrona County International Airport is located about twenty miles west of Casper on the Old West Yellowstone Highway. It is a lonely, desolate two-lane highway on its way to nowhere. The sign for the airport terminal seemed larger than the terminal itself, which in those days had only one ticket counter and two gates.

The weather was cold and snowy, a typical January in Casper. The reason I was making this trip to the airport was to meet Don Angelica and escort him back to Mr. Jones' house for the big meeting of minds. The musical show was to be finalized that weekend. The new opener, *Hallelujah Trail*, was already in rehearsal, and the decision had been made to keep *Battle Hymn of the Republic, Black Saddle,* and *Tumbling Tumble Weeds* from the previous year.

Retaining portions of a drum corps' show from one year to another was quite common in those days; in fact it wasn't that uncommon for an entire show to be repeated from one year to the next.

Don Angelica had a special way of selling his musical ideas for the show by humming or singing their key phrases or "hooks" over and over, but of course, always with an impeccable sense of good taste, timing, and nonchalance. As we drove Don would cleverly couch each of these little sound bites between bits of conversational fun and games, or he might out and out just sing out the phrase. At any rate, by the time we pulled up in front of Mr. Jones' house, the tunes that Don would propose that evening were already floating around inside my head.

Upon arriving at Mr. Jones' I noticed the same little snippets of phrase floating around the house as Don went from room to room. Don was a very good salesman. In the midst of an enjoyable evening, masquerading as a staff meeting, Don's suggestions of *Never My Love* and *Up Up and Away* for the new concert, and a rousing rendition of *American Salute* for the closer were unanimously approved by all present.

1968 was a great year for drum and bugle corps brass sections. Both the American Legion and VFW congresses had approved the G-F bugle in 1967. The difference between the G-D and G-F bugle was huge. The G-D bugle had several key notes missing in its lower register namely A, F, and E, as well as low B, Bb, and A, all of which existed on the G-F instrument. We did lose a low D and an even lower G but you can't have everything.

The G-D instrument was inherently out of tune, and difficult to play due to large changes of resistance between "open" notes and "valve" notes. But in defense of the G-D bugle, it was the only configuration possible that would allow a major scale to be played with only one valve. Somebody must have figured that out on a trumpet!

1968 was my second year of teaching class A drum and bugle corps. The information gathered during the 1967 season from listening to Mr. Jones, observing other drum corps, paying attention to what other instructors had to say, and from speaking with knowledgeable judges, spurred me on to develop a few ideas of my own about creating the ultimate hornline.

Number one, I had always known that teaching one on one was extremely important. It allowed one to get down to the nitty gritty aspects of brass playing, and at the same time answer questions that might not otherwise be asked.

But where I really wanted to spend more time was in warm-up situations. I wanted to work the ensemble's sound. I wrote a few chord sequences and scale patterns that took advantage of the new lower register on the G-F bugle. In this way I could work the line in the mid to low register where it was easier for the performers to relax and produce good quality sound for longer periods of time. In this way we could work on uniformity of articulation, dynamics and phrasing without undue fatigue from constant high register playing. Mid to low register playing also helped open and warm the sound.

In addition to my work with the ensemble I spent many hours in private study, becoming familiar with the various instruments of the ensemble to improve my understanding of what it took to create a good quality of sound on each. Playing a French horn, bass baritone, or contrabass was a very different proposition from playing a soprano or mellophone, and I discovered that I had a lot of practicing to do if I was to contribute good, productive information on these other instruments.

Mr. Jones was able to secure a strobe for me to use. A strobe is a device used to measure pitch, and I would sit for hours with each of the ensemble's instruments, watching the strobe's response in order to learn about proper tuning and producing consistently clear pitches. One after another I tuned each instrument to the strobe and after they were all done I took measurements of where the tuning slides ended up. I was sure that this experiment afforded me important information but I didn't yet understand exactly what that information was, nor did I know how to put it to use. I was searching and exploring the terrain.

The corps had also supplied me with a small variable pitch tone generator that ran on batteries and could be used outdoors as an aid in the general tuning of the line. The idea of fine intonation being the cornerstone of good ensemble playing was beginning to take hold in my approach to teaching.

* * *

One day Fred Sanford said that he wanted to come over and hear my stereo system. I had been telling him all about it and we finally had the opportunity. In those days a good stereo was really something special, especially in Casper, Wyoming.

My room at the Carrs' house was small. I had the stereo equipment on top of an old upright piano. I will never forget Fred's expression when he first heard the opening bars to *Jupiter* from *The Planets* by Gustav Holst. It wasn't the sound of the stereo so much as the music itself that captured Fred's attention. He became absorbed in the sounds. He listened to the whole recording of *The Planets*. He had never heard anything like it. I chose some Copland for him to listen to and I played some Stravinsky. Fred was in heaven.

Fred was attending San Jose State College that semester and was involved with teaching a local drum corps from Santa Clara along with Pete Emmons. He was also marching his age-out year with the Troopers. Fred talked to me about the possibility of my coming out to San Jose in the fall to attend college at San Jose State, and maybe do some teaching with his new corps from Santa Clara, The Vanguard.

I knew I would have to go somewhere other than Casper College to finish my degree in music because Casper College was only a two year program. So I told Fred that I would think about it. But to tell the truth it already sounded like a good idea.

Edie and I were still going out and happily enjoying our time together. I had brought her some trendy clothes back from my trip to New York. My good friend Johnny Guarino's wife Cecilia had insisted that we go downtown and have some fun finding a few things for Edie to wear. When I presented Edie with the things Cecilia and I had chosen for her she was instantly taken with the styles and picked several of the pieces to wear in a photo shoot for a special fashion edition of the Casper Star Tribune.

* * *

The more I got to know Edie's mom the more I liked her. Edie's mom was terrific. Her name was Sandra and she was a reporter for the Casper Star Tribune. She went out of her way to make me feel welcome when I came to visit Edie. I only had the chance to meet Edie's father once in a while when he wasn't out of town. He was a hard working carpenter and seemed to keep pretty busy.

Friday night at the Booth house was a time for getting together. Mrs. Booth would supply the Pepsi cola, potato chips and plenty of talk, deep discussions about you name it, and as always there was plenty of music. All three of Edie's brothers Jim, Ted, and Marv played guitar and sang. And in 1968 a guy who could play guitar and sing had his pick of the best pop music ever produced. The Booth home on Melrose Street was a warm, welcoming and wonderful place.

* * *

Toward the end of the spring semester I flew out to San Jose to visit Fred Sanford and get myself all set up for the fall term. I registered at San Jose State and accompanied Fred to his dorm room where he proceeded to pay me back in kind. He handed me a set of Koss earphones and cued up the newest album of Paul Simon and Art Garfunkel entitled Old Friends. The music was fresh, clean, and vibrant. It painted heartfelt scenes through the use of pitch, rhythm, and rhyme. It was Fred's favorite album of the week!

Fred also introduced me to Gail Royer who was the director of the Vanguard Drum and Bugle Corps. Gail and I spoke briefly about the possibility of my working with the corps in the fall, then Fred took me out for some hot California cuisine: Taco Bell! It was one of Fred's favorite fast food places to frequent. I am not a fast food kind of guy so I promised myself that I would only go to Taco Bell if I went with Fred.

That evening Fred and I set off for Casper in Fred's noisy little Volkswagen. The first of two strange occurrences of the trip happened while we were headed north on highway 680. We passed a sign indicating the exit for Concord, California, and as we passed the sign I had the oddest feeling of premonition and asked Fred if there was a drum corps from Concord. He said he didn't know of any, but I can still see the sign receding into the darkness off to the side of the road. Some kind of transpositional foreshadowing I suppose.

The second strange incident occurred when I was suddenly awakened out of a deep sleep by a very loud noise and the crazed image of Fred frantically beeping the car's horn and yelling at the top of his lungs.

We were speeding across the Utah salt flats, windows wide open, maybe ninety degrees out, racing two huge Diesel engines pounding down the track pulling freight. The train was only about fifteen feet away and just as I noticed the engineer waving at Fred the engineer blew his whistle and Fred's whole face burst into a big happy grin from ear to ear. It appeared that Fred really liked trains.

For his age out year with the Troopers, Fred had a great new idea. Tuned, single headed, tonal bass drums were his choice for the percussion feature of the 1968 season; the Troopers drum line was going to be right up with the times.

Jim McDaniels, a big boy to begin with, wore two gigantic single headed base drums mounted horizontally on an extra strong harness. No one dared get within fifteen feet of him. He was a moving disaster on the field of competition. Fred Sanford was wearing a harness of three smaller cut away bass drums.

Mr. Jones found it necessary to separate both Jim and Fred from the rest of the corps by marching them close to the sideline nearest the stands. This was okay except for the fact that it had a very unusual effect on the recordings of the Troopers that year. In those days the microphones for recording the corps were lined up along the sideline nearest the stands, right where Fred and Jim performed their "quint" essential show. Consequently the recordings featured Fred and Jim and little else. Not good for the recordings but entertaining for the times.

* * *

Edie's mom Sandra came along on the national's tour that year as a chaperone. The tour happened to take the corps through New York City and Mr. Jones said I could use the staff car to go and visit my family. So Edie, Mrs. Booth and I went off to the Bronx to meet the rest of the Meehans.

We were on our way to the same small four room apartment on Kingsbridge Avenue that I had grown up in, where once upon a time my Mom and Dad, big brother Bill, yours truly, younger brother Donald, sister Joan and youngest brother Tom all lived together with a dog, a parakeet, and one tiny bathroom. Cozy was not the word.

The whole family showed up at the house. Mom had made a tasty array of foods and everyone wanted to talk to Edie and Mrs. Booth. Sandra had just recently interviewed John Wayne on the set of his new motion picture Hellfighters.

It was truly wonderful to see everyone so bubbly and alive. We only had a few hours to chitchat and have fun before we were off to Boston.

* * *

The Troopers won the CYO championship that year and I must admit that it was quite a thrill.

It was my first time!

I'd never been part of anything that had gone on to win a title. I was no longer connected to the earth. I felt a bolt of energy flash through my body from my feet up and out the top of my head. I was standing on top of the world getting my hand shook, and my back slapped. And when all was said and done I felt wrung out, weak, and at peace.

The Kilties and the Royalairs were tied for fourth place in the preliminary competition at VFW Nationals that year with the Cavaliers in third, Troopers in second, and the Des Plains Vanguard in first. In those days the preliminary competition was always held during the hottest part of the day, and it was a requirement that all shows be shortened due to time considerations. This could have accounted for skewed scores depending on how the shows had been adjusted to meet the timing criteria, and, whether the performers remembered to correctly perform the changes in the shortened prelim show.

In the final competition the Royalairs placed fifth, Des Plains Vanguard fourth, Troopers third, Cavaliers second and the Kilties won the show.

The Kilties won high brass, high general effect, tied St. Joes Batavia for high percussion, and placed fifth in marching.

The Kilties were far and away the brass line of the year. I cherish the few times I had the pleasure of hearing them live. Their sound was light, free, and resonant. The Kilties presented a whole new level of achievement in brass performance. Ken Norman, drill writer, instructor, arranger and general guru of all things brass, gave us all a glimpse into the future and a taste of what was possible.

The Kilties put together back-to-back VFW titles in 1968 and 1969 with virtually the exact same show!

Unheard of! But extremely well deserved.

With the close of the 1968 drum corps season came the opening of my new life in sunny California.

Chapter 6
1969 Troopers, Santa Clara, Wedding Day

Casper, Wyoming had been a big change from New York City, but here I was in San Jose, California in the fall of 1968 and I felt like I was in another world. The easygoing weather, the easygoing lifestyle, living in an apartment with Fred Sanford and Pete Emmons, attending classes at San Jose State, teaching the Vanguard, trips back and forth to Wyoming, practicing trumpet, working with the San Jose State Marching Band; it was an absolute dream come true. I was inundated with exhilaration. Life was a giant candy store. There was so much to do, so much to experience, so much to learn, and so many wonderful people to get to know.

That year the Vanguard had Don Angelica come out to California to help with song selection and show design. The Vanguard show for that year was diverse: *Procession of the Nobles, Chester Overture, Turkey Lurkey Time, Promises, Promises, Mas Que Nada, You Make Me So Very Happy,* and *By the Time I Get To Phoenix.* It was very different repertoire from what the Troopers would have chosen.

The Vanguard had only been together for one year, and the performers did not yet possess much in the way of experience or tradition but it was obvious that Gail Royer was going to change all of that. The corps was managed very well. Rehearsals were run on time and members were kept well informed about coming events and their personal responsibilities.

Brass rehearsals were held in a small band room, no risers, just large enough to fit an arc from wall to wall, corner to corner. As it was in Casper I was the only instructor at brass rehearsals and I didn't have the luxury of practice rooms to break up into sectionals, so we did some individual playing during ensemble rehearsals. It took a while for the brass players to get used to the idea of performing in front of each other but in the long run they improved and gained a sense of fun and confidence about the task.

There were a few really fine players in the Vanguard brass section, and they reminded me of my friends back on the east coast who played because they loved to play. I had a great deal of respect for those who were willing to lay it out on the line and learn from it.

The most telling part of a Vanguard rehearsal was when the corps came together at the end, always outside, Fred and I would do a little ensemble work and then the brass and percussion would play through the entire routine with the color guard performing all of the flag and rifle work.

This was where Pete Emmons instilled the traditional Vanguard posture and soldier like attention to duty. Who could you possibly imagine shouting out the commands more decisively than the celebrated drum major of the world champion Casper Troopers?

The corps improved noticeably from week to week but the most obvious improvement was in the percussion section. They were beginning to display a quality of sound that was musical in a way that I had never heard before in drum corps. It wasn't just the new tonal sounds, it was texture and balance, dynamics, and musical understanding that I was hearing, and that was what Fred was teaching.

* * *

During the winter of 1968 Mike Duffy arrived in Casper. He was there to write a few new arrangements, and to help with the week-to-week instruction of the hornline while I was attending school in California.

Mike was a talented guy. He played trumpet with great enthusiasm and he played piano as though he had played it all his life. He could improvise a tune as well as anyone. When it finally came time to arrange the tunes for the 1969 Troopers' show it went something like this.

Mike and I would sit down and he would improvise a phrase at the piano, at least eight different ways and then, he would turn to me and say, "Which one do you like the best?" and I would say, "I can't decide, do it again" and he would play another eight improvisations and I would say, "Which one do you like Mike?" and he would say, "Well, I kind of like some of this one and some of that" and as he said it he would put the two variations together at the piano. It was a long but fun process and judging from the crowd response that year it worked very well.

The Troopers repertoire in 1969 was *Hang 'em High,* a new improved *Battle Hymn of the Republic, Aquarius, Let the Sunshine In, Scarborough Fair, Tumbling Tumbleweeds, Sounds of Silence,* and *When Johnny Comes Marching Home.* It was a really good show, and Mike's new arrangements were exactly what the corps needed. They were colorful, rich, and lively, with lots of good parts for all. It was great to have someone like Mike around to kibitz with and share teaching responsibilities. Mike stayed with the Troopers through May of 1970.

* * *

Edie and I were engaged to be married in the spring of 1969 and we tied the knot on July 19th between tours. It was a full Trooper wedding. Fred Sanford was my best man and Edie's cousin Joan was the maid of honor. As we left the church the Trooper color guard saluted us with a long archway of flags and rifles.

The brass and percussion, in full uniform, (they changed clothes in the parking lot to the surprise of all the little Greek ladies) played a rousing rendition of Battle Hymn of the Republic.

Almost all of my family was there. They had taken the train out from New York. Mom and Dad, brother Donald and his wife Kitty, sister Joan and brother Tom all had tall stories to tell of their railway adventure west.

Edie and I were going to honeymoon in Yellowstone Park. We had just five days before we had to be back for nationals tour (Edie was still in the color guard). We hopped into our little red Sunbeam, said good-bye to all, and went happily and speedily on our way.

I guess the tealeaf reader in New York had gotten it right on all counts. I found my fortune and I married me a beautiful wife in the wild and woolly west.

* * *

1969 was a great year for the Casper Troopers. I thought the brass sound was the best so far, perhaps due to the fact that it was a three year veteran line. It's always great to have those 19, 20, and 21 year olds in the line who have been around for a while and understand what has to be done.

Mr. Jones outdid himself on the show design that year. The drill for *When Johnny Comes Marching Home* was an architect's dream. In order for the drill to work, the corps had to have absolute control over step size, which was seven steps every five yards.

"If the step size is perfect, well then Katie bar the door!" was what Mr. Jones would say before having the whole corps close their eyes and march a company front one hundred yards at elbow contact. In the center of the company front was one of the color guard girls whose responsibility it was to hit the yard line precisely every seven steps with a smooth even gait. Her eyes were open.

The *Johnny Comes Marching Home* drill and music was one of the finest total effect productions I have ever witnessed on the drum corps field. If you would like to hear how the crowd reacted to this moment of history order the 1969 Fleetwood recording of the Troopers at CYO Nationals. You can hear the crowd roar when the company front hits the twenty-yard line on its way to victory.

The Troopers also won the World Open Championship that year and placed third at the VFW Nationals in Philadelphia.

The Santa Clara Vanguard went all the way to the east coast in 1969 and competed in the World Open Championship. They made it into the finals and placed 9th. Gail Royer, following in Mr. Jones' footsteps, took the corps to Washington, D.C. and New York City for a bit of east coast culture and well deserved R 'n R.

When the Troopers arrived back in Casper, Edie and I packed up the Sunbeam, said our goodbyes to one and all, and headed off into the sunset toward our new life together in the California sun.

Chapter 7
1970 Troopers and Santa Clara - Winners

Edie and I were just getting settled in our little apartment in San Jose, which was well situated, about fifteen minutes from anywhere we needed to go.

I'll never forget our first marital problem.

We were at the super market buying things for our new home when we were confronted with a stunning realization. The dialog went something like this: I said, "How about spaghetti for dinner?" and Edie said, "Okay, I'll get the Chef Boyardee" and I said, "Are you kidding? I wouldn't eat that stuff on a bet!" then Edie said, "Well, that's what my mother always got when she went to the store" so I replied, "Let's make the spaghetti fresh, what do you suppose makes the sauce red, carrots?"

True story!

I was entering my fourth year teaching class A drum and bugle corps, and the only thing I knew for certain was that I had a long way to go before I could create the absolute ultimate in competitive brass performance.

How does one go about inspiring individuals to be the very best? What musical environment will bring about a consistent sense of awareness in the areas of tempo, dynamics and style? And how does one accurately control the pitch of sixty brass instruments in varying degrees of temperature, humidity and altitude?

These were questions I wanted answers to and I knew the information would not be found between the covers of any single book. Finding the answers would eventually take countless hours of research in psychology, musicianship, and acoustics. And due to my happy situation as newlywed, full time student, performer, brass instructor, and traveling clinician, it was going to be a long while before I could do the necessary bookwork.

As I revisit these days of my life I realize that there was no time put aside to internally process all of the emotional and situational experiences life was throwing my way. The nice part was that I thoroughly enjoyed all of it.

But I was spread too thin and didn't realize it. There was never quite enough time left over for sleep, and certainly no time at all for reverie or emotional assimilation. I now know what I didn't realize back then. I was inescapably steaming toward a personal train wreck that would shake me to my very core.

* * *

Edie was hired by Gail Royer to work with the Vanguard winter color guard. She had spent eight years in the Troopers' color guard learning from the master himself about posture and carriage, and she knew very well how to give commands, and keep the guard's focus where it needed to be. In every way Edie was a wonderful model for the girls in the guard to emulate. Both her posture and attitude radiated self-confidence. She was straightforward and demanding, exacting yet understanding. It was a joy to watch Edie in action.

The Vanguard show for 1970 had a style that foretold the future of the corps. The combination of Broadway and the classics became a Santa Clara tradition. That year the show consisted of the introduction, *Festive Overture*, *Procession of the Nobles* for the opener, *Chester Overture* for color presentation, *Miracle of Miracles*, *Matchmaker*, *Fiddler on the Roof*, and *If I were a Rich Man* for the concert and production package, and for the closer, *Bridge over Troubled Water*. It was a good show, and the corps was beginning to project the image of class and precision that it eventually became famous for.

Pete Emmons, Fred Sanford, and Edie Booth were three of Jim Jones' finest students and they imparted to the members of the Vanguard that which Mr. Jones had bestowed upon them, namely the will to win and the strength of character to perform at their best no matter what the odds.

(I sometimes wonder how different my life and many other lives would have been if not for Jim Jones' desire to create a drum and bugle corps for the young people of Casper, Wyoming to experience and enjoy.)

* * *

The Troopers musical show for 1970 stayed much the same as the year before with the exceptions of *Gary Owen March* and *Turkey in the Straw* replacing *Tumbling Tumble Weeds*, and *How the West Was Won* replacing the *Sounds of Silence*.

We had a new staff member join us that year by the name of Joe Marrella. Mr. Jones asked Joe to come to Casper and work with the percussion section for the 1970 season, so Joe commuted by air from New Jersey to Denver, and then stagecoach from Denver to Casper for the camp weekends. His style of teaching was fun, focused, functional, and transformative. He was an inspirational teacher, who not only affected the percussion section, but the whole corps as well, staff included. As far as Joe Marrella was concerned there is always an up side, and that is the only side worth considering.

* * *

In the early spring of 1970, Edie and I drove from San Jose to the central valley of California and visited a kennel where they raised Great Danes. The dogs were so beautiful and graceful that we decided there on the spot to take the cutest puppy of all home with us.

Her name was Majestic Minka and she was the runt of the litter. Her ears had recently been clipped and she wore them up on top of her head suspended by a rack. She was the most adorable creature either Edie or I had ever seen. We named her Daphne. We really tried our best with the ear rack but the top two inches of her left ear always fell over and made her look slightly quizzical.

Chapter 8
Drum Corps Perspective

There is no doubt in my mind that 1970 was the cornerstone year in the history of my life. As I hear the kids say these days, "it was all good."

The Casper Troopers had the best competitive season of their 13-year history. They won virtually all of their shows including World Open, CYO Nationals, and VFW Nationals. The Santa Clara Vanguard also had a very successful season winning the North American Open and the American Legion National title. Edie and I celebrated our first anniversary, and our son John was born to us during a cold Casper snowstorm in December of that same wonderful and exciting year.

* * *

In retrospect, 1970 marked the end of an era for drum and bugle corps. Allow me to explain.

From the start of what I consider the age of modern drum corps, beginning somewhere around 1947, the VFW and American Legion National Championships were completely dominated by east coast drum corps. The Holy Name Cadets of Garfield New Jersey, St. Vincent Cadets of Bayonne New Jersey, the Blessed Sacrament Golden Knights of Newark New Jersey, and the Osmond Cadets from Philadelphia Pennsylvania had been the major players.

Then in 1957, ten years later, a drum corps from the midwest broke the eastern strong hold on the VFW title. From that point onward midwest drum corps, namely the Chicago Cavaliers, The Racine Kilties, and the Chicago Royalairs won all but two VFW National Championships.

That is until 1966, nine years later, when a little known drum and bugle corps from way out west, the Casper Troopers, convoyed into Jersey City, New Jersey and stole the VFW title right out from under everyone's nose.

East coast drum corps had held a tight rein on the American Legion National title until 1965 when the title fell firmly into the hands of the Chicago Royalairs. Drum corps domination was definitely moving west.

To understand what eventually happened to drum and bugle corps realize that in order to win a major competition like the VFW, a corps had to compete in enough local and regional shows to be well prepared for their chance at the top prize.

Competing regularly and being evaluated by competent judges was not a problem for the east coast or midwest corps because a multitude of well established local competitions were already being sponsored on a regular basis. But way out west in Casper, Wyoming, Mr. Jim Jones and his Troopers had a very different situation.

The Troopers were located a thousand miles from the nearest competition. That meant two days' travel to get to the competition area and two days to return home. It was a logistical nightmare. It took money and equipment to transport one hundred and fifty people two thousand miles, and in those days if you didn't win the competition you didn't win any prize money. Even if you did win the competition, you didn't win much prize money. So Jim Jones, after 13 years of trying to make it work on a logistical basis, decided to take the bull by the horns.

From the time the Troopers returned home from the 1970 championship tour, Mr. Jones devoted himself to the task of creating what would eventually become Drum Corps International. He wanted to bring about an atmosphere of cooperation and sharing between "staunch rivals" so the idiom of drum and bugle corps would finally be in command of its own destiny.

* * *

When the Santa Clara Vanguard won the American Legion title in 1970, it marked the beginning of California's complete domination of the drum corps world, and that domination continued for the next 13 years with one striking exception: the notorious capturing of the DCI World Championship in 1975 by the Madison Scouts of Madison, Wisconsin.

I say notorious because of the sudden axe-like disqualification of the Hawthorne Muchachos of Hawthorne, New Jersey from DCI competition. The Muchachos were considered by many to be a strong contender for the top spot at DCI that year but were cruelly and disdainfully disqualified from competition upon completion of their preliminary performance at the World Championships in Philadelphia.

They were disqualified immediately upon leaving the competition field for having an overage member in their ranks. The score sheets from their preliminary performance were destroyed before anyone had a chance to see them. It was as though the corps had been ripped from the fabric of drum and bugle corps society. Now you see them, now you don't. It was a bad day for drum and bugle corps.

This same disqualification ploy was used again two years later in 1977, but this time the east coast corps involved, namely the Bayonne Bridgemen, obtained a court ordered injunction that allowed the corps to at least perform their show in the final competition.

So 1970 marked not only the end of midwest and east coast drum corps domination, it marked the beginning of California supremacy and ushered in the beginning of World Class touring drum corps.

* * *

It was not until 1983 that an east coast drum corps would succeed, for the first time ever, in capturing the DCI World title. And that was exactly twenty-three years since the last east coast drum corps brought home the VFW National title in 1960.

Twenty-three years was a long time to wait!

Chapter 9
1971 Troopers - Midwest Combine

It was January 1971. A typically cold, windy, Casper, Wyoming winter and I found it absolutely invigorating. I had taken a job in an office machine repair shop on the old C Y Strip. I made use of the expertise I had gathered while working for the Burroughs Corporation in New York City eight years earlier. Luckily, there was another fellow working in the shop who knew what he was doing, and he was nice enough to help me get my mind back into the workings of the machines. He told me he rabbit hunted on weekends and asked if I would like to try my hand at it.

I'll never forget the few times I went along with Ken to hunt those pesky rabbits. Dressed in a one-piece snowsuit with my trusty Great Dane Daphne at my side, Ken and I drove out to Powder River, Wyoming, which seemed to be nothing more than a mail drop, and found ourselves in a pristine snowscape of rugged Wyoming prairie land.

A pure white blanket of freshly fallen snow lay there before us, sparkling under a cold, distant sun in a huge cornflower blue sky. Off in the distance stood rough, mountainous red rock formations trimmed lightly with a dusting of snow borders.

As we entered the terrain we encountered a warren of gullies and troughs about six feet high and eight feet wide. They channeled through the terrain in such a way that you never knew what was lurking around the next bend.

I heard and felt the crunch of snow under foot as I had never heard or felt it before. The sound and feel created a kind of visceral sensation deep inside that reminded me of walking up a creaky set of stairs late at night. But other than the crunch of snow under foot and the sounds of

Daphne's panting there was nothing. There was no ambient noise. The snow seemed to soak up sound like a sponge.

So when the rabbit bolted from its hidey-hole it created an audio-visual strike on the senses. Daphne had been running free having a great old time until the first shot was fired. The sudden sound of the rifle's report shattered the still air and Daphne froze in place. It was then that I heard Ken say softly, "missed." Daphne took off again but kept an eye on Ken from then on.

I think we drove out to Powder River two or three times in all. What I remember vividly was that the first time I actually shot and killed a rabbit was the last time I ever went. It wasn't like fishing where you could take the hook out of the fish's mouth and throw it back into its watery existence unharmed. This was very final for the rabbit and it didn't feel like the kind of thing I wanted to do. But I loved the adventure of it all.

* * *

Edie, John, Daphne, and I were living in a small two-bedroom house in the southeast section of Casper. It was quiet and open, and had a great view of Casper Mountain.

That year I was teaching both the Trooper A and B corps brass sections during evenings and weekends, and working in the office machine repair shop during the weekdays.

Mr. Jones was hard at work getting the "combine" together. The combine was to be a consortium of top drum and bugle corps banding together in the style of the Three Musketeers: "all for one and one for all."

The five corps chosen to make up the combine were the Casper Troopers, Chicago Cavaliers, Madison Scouts, La Crosse Blue Stars, and Santa Clara Vanguard. The idea was that these five corps would consolidate in their endeavors to establish particulars about time, date, place and prize money when speaking with show sponsors.

While Mr. Jones was championing his combine cause over the phone with directors of the other corps, he and Don Whiteley were laying the groundwork for a series of three competitions to be held right in Mr. Jones' own backyard. This series of shows was known as Drums Along the Rockies and would have its inaugural run in June of 1971. Mr. Jones was also planning a new drum corps publication with Don Whiteley that would eventually be known as Drum Corps World.

As you can see, Mr. Jones was a shaker and mover. He started a drum and bugle corps in the middle of nowhere and brought it to the pinnacle of excellence twice in thirteen years. He knew how to get things done. He was a master at getting people motivated to do what it was he wanted to do. By the time Mr. Jones was done explaining what he wanted to have happen he had people thinking it was their idea to do it in the first place.

That year the corps was going to play Holst's *March in Eb* for the opening of the show, *Battle Hymn* for color presentation, *Pops Hoe-down*, and *William Tell Overture* for production number and concert.

And this was where the show broke tradition.

The whole second half of the show was a blow-by-blow account of a battle between the US Cavalry and the American Indians. The music used to portray the western tableau was derived from *Wagon Wheels*, along with incidental music from *How the West Was Won* and *Dingus Magee*. This was one of the first examples of a "story line" show, some-what like the '71 Cavaliers' Circus Show and the '71 Madison Scouts' Alice in Wonderland Show.

* * *

Due to the fact that it was all new music, except for Battle Hymn, I asked Mr. Jones if I could bring John Gates in from the Blue Stars to do a brass clinic with us. I had attended a clinic John gave at the last rules congress and I was eager to learn more, and to more fully understand that which I had previously observed.

John's clinic had been focused on brass instrument tuning. He used a strobe tuner and a soprano bugle to demonstrate the relationship be-tween the pitch and tone of a given sound. He began by tuning his in-strument to the pitch of the strobe, adjusting the tuning slide to bring about a clear resonant tone with the proper pitch.

He then pulled the tuning slide out about a half-inch and played the exact same pitch as he had before. The difference between the first note and the second note was one of tone quality. The second note lacked the clarity and resonance of the first. The second note was stuffy and tight.

The second note registered the same pitch as the first note but it presented a very different tone quality!

Mr. Gates then pushed the slide in about an inch and once again played the same pitch. Just as it had before the tone quality suffered greatly but the pitch remained the same. He then tuned the instrument properly by adjusting the tuning slide until the pitch was correct and the tone quality was again clear and resonant.

The experience had a similar effect to that of witnessing a magic trick being performed: everything seems clear and understandable until it comes to the end of the trick. Then suddenly, the audience is not quite sure of what has transpired before their eyes, or precisely how they were manipulated, but they know quite well that the magician knows something that they do not.

One of the many things I learned from John Gates was that everything goes easily when you understand what it is that you are doing. John Gates understood what was necessary when it came to putting a fine brass ensemble together, and he endeavored to convey what he could to my hungry mind. But due to my naive state of unenlightened awareness I was not yet able to use this information to its fullest extent.

* * *

For one reason or another the Troopers never practiced or performed on grass during the winter and spring of 1971. When weather permitted, they practiced outside on a concrete parking lot where there was no high vantage point from which to view or hear the corps. So on the day of the corps' first show, which was being held for the first time ever in Casper Wyoming, we had the good fortune to do a short rehearsal at the Natrona County High School Stadium.

It was early morning. We were extremely lucky to be rehearsing at the contest site because the grounds crews in Casper were manically protective of their turf. We anxiously gathered upstairs to see what had been wrought over the last nine months.

It became immediately apparent, from the very first note, that there was a big problem! I had to strain to hear the brass. They were not projecting the sound. They sounded tentative. I remember thinking to myself "Oh no, what do I do now?"

The hornline had a nice sound and they knew their music but they would need to play louder and project their musical image up to the top of the stands. It was a very young hornline. They had been rehearsed indoors at the Natrona County Fairgrounds Industrial Building throughout the winter and had gone outdoors only recently. And as I said before, this was their first time on grass.

There is a big difference between playing on asphalt and playing on grass. When you play on asphalt, you get an inordinate amount of feedback, which bolsters your self-confidence and provides a false sense of security. But when you play on grass there is no feedback. You feel as though you're playing all by yourself, which has a tendency to make you want to hold back.

The drum corps competing with the Troopers in the first show ever of Drums Along the Rockies in Casper, were the Madison Scouts, Argonne Rebels, Hutchinson Sky Riders, and Santa Clara Vanguard.

We did okay at the show that night, if taking second place to the Santa Clara Vanguard could be considered okay, but we were warned by the judges that the corps would have to project the show with a sense of command and presence. They had to "sell it to the audience."

The next morning we left for Cheyenne, which was about three hours south on interstate twenty-five. The idea was to rehearse when we arrived in town.

There was always time for rehearsal!

So I began to think about what I could do to help our cause. I couldn't believe how many ideas began generating in my mind. Wow! I borrowed a writing tablet and began taking notes of what I was thinking.

The rehearsal field in Cheyenne was a neglected football field with a high hill to one side allowing a good view of the corps from above. Mr. Jones rehearsed, and rehearsed, and rehearsed. Now that he was on tour he could devote himself to teaching and instilling his own brand of motivation, which simply stated was, no room for error.

Setting up the combine and coordinating the Drums Along the Rockies tour had taken its toll on Mr. Jones' time throughout the winter and spring. But now that it was contest season, and there were no telephone calls to interrupt him (this was long before cell phones), he could do what he liked to do best, and that was rehearse.

That night the reigning national champion Casper Troopers placed fourth, behind the Santa Clara Vanguard, the Madison Scouts, and the Argonne Rebels. This was definitely not good. That night, after the show, Mr. Jones and the corps rehearsed out on the blacktop with parents providing light from their cars. The amazing thing was that the kids in the corps took it all in stride and never faltered. The older members had been there before and the younger ones were learning what it was to be a Trooper. It took hard work, dedication, and an unfailing attitude of determination to please Mr. Jones. And pleasing Mr. Jones was what the Troopers all wished to do.

After the corps had finally settled down that evening, and the lights were turned out, my son John, at seven months old, decided that he needed to cry. And he cried, and he cried, and he cried. We were in a small room adjacent to the gymnasium where the corps was trying to sleep. John cried solid for two hours straight. He had never cried like that before and has never cried like that since. Fourth place can be absolutely devastating to a true competitor.

The next day I was given a short block of time with the brass section. I explained to them the need to keep a clear head and maintain focus on their intention to perform at their best.

To bring the point home I outlined a fifteen-minute exercise to be performed at their highest level of achievement. They were to stand at attention for fifteen minutes, without moving, keeping their minds free of distraction while intensely focusing their awareness on the performance of their show. I told them that they should see this exercise as an opportunity to seize control of their mind and body during difficult situations, and, that if anyone was going to faint, they should not fall on their instrument.

I informed the contra bass section that they could put their instruments down due to their heavy weight but they refused saying that if everyone else was going to hold their instrument at attention then they would too.

I am proud to tell you that every last player performed the exercise like a proverbial trooper and when the grueling fifteen minutes had been accomplished each and every one of them looked as though they had personally faced down a mental demon or two.

That evening the Troopers charged back into second place with only nine tenths of a point separating them from the Vanguard.

* * *

The rest of the 1971 season proved to be an uphill battle but the corps worked as hard as any I have ever seen and managed to place second at VFW Nationals behind, you guessed it, the new guys on the block, The Santa Clara Vanguard.

Chapter 10
1972 Troopers - First DCI

In September of 1971 we were once again loading the family car with all the usual items in preparation for our relocation to Laramie, Wyoming. Our family was growing! No more two-seater Sunbeam Alpine. We were now sporting a 1960 Volkswagen bus. Oh how things change.

We were off to the University of Wyoming to study advanced calf roping, and for me to finish my teaching degree. I had one and a half years of classes and student teaching left before completing my bachelor's in music education.

We found a small two-bedroom house located approximately 50 yards from the University of Wyoming football stadium. Since I would be involved with the marching band, I thought that was pretty good planning, that is until football season came around.

On game days, hordes of howling gridiron enthusiasts would stampede through our front yard on their way to the game, and then, about three hours later they would come mooing their way back out. This 'in-and-out' parade occured only inches from our living room window. You could always tell who won the game by the crowd's mood on the way out.

* * *

All in all it was a rough and tumble year.

There was family time, class time, practice time, study time, performance time (I actually toured Wyoming with the University of Wyoming concert band performing the Doc Severinsen arrangement of the theme from *Love Story,* in which I played Doc) and travel time to and from Casper for Trooper rehearsals and family time with Yia Yia (Edie's mom).

* * *

I loved being a dad and was more than willing to swap study time for being with John time. We would go for walks. John was coming up on one year old and whatever John found interesting would require a complete stop and consequent investigation. I was strictly a bystander who received an occasional questioning glance from John as he looked over a pinecone, rock or stick.

At one year old there wasn't a huge amount of meaningful verbal communication going on. The feeling I had while accompanying my year old son on a discovery walk was rather primitive in nature: intensely in the moment; fully absorbed in the purely sense oriented activity of search and discover.

Daphne the Great Dane would sometimes accompany John and me on our walks. When John would stop to investigate something, Daphne would sit, snort, and manage to look totally bored. I guess she was accustomed to that primitive, natural state.

To this day, I can still recall with absolute clarity, myself, at about one year old, sitting on the kitchen floor playing with pots and pans, making sounds of pings and pangs, playing with the shapes and weights, stacking pots inside of one another, and wearing them on my head. Totally in the moment: primitive, fun, productive, and completely self motivated.

Now, that was life… free and unfettered! One hundred percent awareness and mental presence intensely focused in the moment where future becomes present; the only moment in which you can actually get something done: the moment of now, the moment of action.

Years later I wrote this poem to express how I felt about presence of mind and living fully in the present moment.

Presence of mind is my favorite topic
It separates the men from the boys
It demonstrates power
Administers on demand
Emanates wisdom
Encapsulates command
Presence of mind is not a rock band
It is home base for your mental powers
It is your trusty dog at your side
Panting away… Awaiting your pleasure
Presence of mind is just plain being there
Along for the ride with nothing to hide
Meeting the future head on
As it come crashing into the present
Presence of mind is life at its fullest
Spontaneous and fluid
Immediate, exciting, and
Always first nighting

* * *

Wintertime can be truly unforgiving in Wyoming.

One cold, crisp Sunday evening in mid January of 1972, Daphne, John, Edie, and I were all snuggled warmly into our Volkswagen bus ready for our run down to Laramie to get ready for spring semester. It was cold, but otherwise clear and dry. There was no wind! That should have tipped us off, but we went happily on our way.

We took highway 220 southwest out of town, which took us out past the Natrona County International Airport, past Alcova Dam, down through Muddy Gap, and on out the Medicine Bow cutoff. The Medicine Bow cutoff is a much shorter route than the alternative but it does take you into Shirley Basin, and then up a straight shot incline that climbs one thousand two hundred feet in six miles to the top of Shirley Rim.

Everything seemed calm that evening as we began our ascent, but as we climbed to about half way up the incline it started to snow. Just flurries at first, but by the time we hit the summit of the rim it was a full blown raging snow storm with a thirty or forty mile per hour cross wind.

This was high plains country where the wind is always brutal and cold. There are no windbreaks along the road because nothing can survive the constant wind of over thirty-five miles per hour.

We actually experienced snow coming up through a hole in the floorboards that I had never noticed before. We had forward visibility of maybe ten feet. The snow poles along the sides of the road were almost not visible. It was a harrowing adventure. I remember seeing Daphne's snoot sticking out over the front seat with her ears straight up.

We drove through those conditions for at least two hours with Edie holding John warmly in her arms. We never saw another vehicle along the road. We never stopped for fear of becoming stuck in the snow. With no means of communication we were completely alone in the middle of frozen nowhere!

Of course we made it through our harrowing experience but the real kicker to the story is that the next day, while Edie was driving through an intersection in Laramie, the engine blew a head gasket and the VW bus stopped dead in its tracks.

* * *

Much of Mr. Jones' surplus time during the period leading up to the 1972 season had been devoted to projects that would ensure the future success of DCI, and being that I spent most of the winter and spring in Laramie, we decided to bring someone in to help with musical arrangements and show concepts.

We asked Mr. Ray Baumgardt from the Madison Scouts to come to Casper and arrange a new rendition of an old Trooper favorite, *Ghost Riders in the Sky*. Ray was very interesting. He knew so much and didn't mind telling me whatever I wanted to know. I had heard his arrangements the year before when the Madison Scouts performed the Alice in Wonderland show. I loved the sound he was able to achieve and wanted to know how he did it. So he told me.

He told me about how he stacked chords using the Hindemith rules of harmonic structure, and he gave me sheet after sheet of articulations and dynamics with complete information for implementation, including graphics. Ray had a method of teaching that if used consistently would produce a wonderful, clear, full, stylized sound from a brass ensemble. I studied it, practiced it and played with it until I understood it from an empirical point of view. Practically every note of Ray's arrangements were marked and fully articulated and therefore stylized. Ray was extremely methodical and it was good for me to experience his particular way of working.

For the color presentation that year, the corps once again played *Battle Hymn of the Republic*, which was followed by a concert rendition of *The Cincinnati Kid*. Two Trooper standards, *When Johnny Comes Marching Home* and *How The West Was Won*, finished out the 1972 show.

* * *

I had an opportunity to witness an Argonne Rebels brass rehearsal that year in an outdoors setting at the fairgrounds in Casper. It was Drums Along the Rockies time again and the Argonne Rebels were rehearsing for the show that evening at the NCHS Stadium. The Troopers had just finished their morning rehearsal so I decided to hang out and watch someone else work for a change, namely Sandra Opie, already legendary among brass enthusiasts for the high quality of her brass ensembles.

But before I tell you about the rehearsal, I would like to make you aware of a little-realized fact. When you win as many shows as the Troopers had won over the past six years you tended to be one of the last if not the last corps to compete in any given competition: the idea of saving the best for last I suppose. Therefore, I never had the opportunity to enjoy the other brass ensembles in the competition, due to the fact that I was always busy with my responsibilities to the Trooper brass section right up until the time they walked out onto the field of competition.

So here I was standing in front of one of the finest drum corps in the world and I was hyped. I had never met or seen Sandra Opie before, but

I had heard that she was really strict when it came to precision. She definitely lived up to her reputation that day. I had seen Don Angelica cut the Trooper brass section four times in a row after having only played the first note of a piece of music, more often than not just to get them to pay closer attention to what they were doing, but this demonstration of zero tolerance I had not been prepared for.

With a strong clear tone the ensemble began playing the introduction to the Barnum and Bailey March. Mrs. Opie cut them. She didn't say anything but I think everyone must have known what was wrong, so they began again and she cut them again, only this time there came a barrage of corrective criticism from Mrs. Opie aimed towards a particular section of the ensemble.

This scenario played out over the next thirty minutes with the ensemble never getting more than a few bars into the piece. To say the least, I felt terribly frustrated. The brass section eventually had the opportunity to play through some of their routine without interruption and they were without doubt a joy to behold, but I vowed on my way home for lunch that I would find a way to create the brass ensemble of my dreams in a more efficient and less musically frustrating way than I had just witnessed. There was no doubt that Mrs. Opie's brass ensemble played with the highest degree of disciplined uniformity I had ever heard from a junior drum and bugle corps, but somehow I felt way down deep that there had to be more to it than that.

And besides, I would never in a million years want to work that hard.

* * *

Toward the end of the 1972 season it was becoming obvious that DCI was a great idea and that the Troopers show was not. One marching judge in particular, who had told Mr. Jones during a critique in 1971 that he thought the western tableau was ridiculous, was now saying that he thought even the tableau would have been better than what he'd seen that evening. He then boisterously declared that he had finally figured a way to judge the intervals of the circle burst as it expanded, meaning that he was hoping to find a lot more "tics" in the Troopers' show the next time around.

I asked Mr. Jones as we left the critique, "What do you do with a judge who is so obviously negative toward the corps?" and his reply was, "Well, in this case I think we'll just have to find something else for him to do."

As far as I know the judge in question stayed with DCI but never judged another DCI show after the 1972 season.

The Troopers placed seventh that year in the preliminary competition at the first DCI World Championships held in Whitewater Wisconsin, but they were able to do that one better by capturing sixth place in the finals.

I'd lucked out and found a great seat up in the stands from which to view the Troopers' performance. It was located just under the press box, so I stayed there to enjoy the top six drum corps in the world as they competed for the first DCI World title.

How cool was that?

I had not experienced that particular treat since the 1966 VFW Nationals in Jersey City when the Troopers took home their first VFW gold!

But this time around there was a difference in my perception, a big difference. I was now capable of appreciating the whole experience of a drum corps show in a broader, and at the same time more specific way. I understood the big picture and the nitty gritty all at the same time. What a great experience it was.

When I think back to that evening, the memories that jump out at me are of the Santa Clara Vanguard and the Anaheim Kingsmen. I found the Vanguard totally engaging. The presentation of their brass, percussion, visual design, and colorguard was a complete delight as demonstrated through their opening productions of *Fanfare and Allegro* by Clifton Williams, and Henry V by Sir William Walton.

The Kingsmen, on the other hand, were shockingly vibrant, hard-hitting, and musically clean as a whistle. I especially enjoyed the brass and colorguard contribution to the *Ritual Fire Dance* production, and was blown away both visually and musically by the fired up percussion solo. The Kingsmen were my choice to win the big one that night and it was nice to see that most of the judges agreed with me. The Kingsmen won high brass, high percussion, placed second in general effect, and took sixth in marching.

Most amazing of all was the fact that even though the Troopers placed sixth overall, the corps still ended up taking first place in the marching caption. It was a tribute to Mr. Jones' talent for getting the job done right.

The overwhelming success of Drum Corps International that year was yet another feather in Mr. Jones' already crowded cap.

Chapter 11
1973 Troopers - Mahler #1

In September of 1972 I was back at the university completing my teaching degree in music education.

I was alone this trip. Edie, John, and Daphne remained back in Casper since I was only going to be in Laramie for half of the semester. The other half semester would be spent student teaching at Kelly Walsh High School in Casper.

I learned to make strange noises on the oboe, the bassoon, the cello, and the violin that semester. I spent time relearning everything I already knew about teaching, and I experienced first hand the "why" of what is really wrong with the educational system in America.

I was enrolled in a condensed course on the psychology of education, and found myself completely hooked by both the teacher and the subject matter. For the next five years I read everything I could get my hands on pertaining to children and learning, from Piaget to Leonard, from Dewey to Samples.

Don't you just love it when that happens!

Back in Casper, Mr. Jones seemed to be his old self again. No more extraneous drum corps stuff going on. DCI and Drums Along the Rockies were established and running. It was time to put the drum corps together and start making plans for the 1973 season.

The music for the show that year was *Ghost Riders in the Sky, Eagle Screams, Black Saddle, Wedding Dance, Thanksgiving Hymn, Day by Day,* and *Battle Hymn of the Republic.*

Ghost Riders was a holdover from the '72 season. *The Eagle Screams* was an original piece by Nelson Riddle, taken from the Phil Silvers' Swinging Brass album. Ray Baumgardt did the arrangement for us.

Black Saddle, Wedding Dance, and the medley of *Thanksgiving Hymn, Day by Day,* and *Battle Hymn of the Republic* were arranged by yours truly. They were my first arrangements and they were the first of only a few. Arranging music, spending all that time alone with a pencil and paper, reminded me too much of doing homework. It was not the way I wanted to spend my time. I don't mind spending my time with a computer these days, but I think that's because I don't have to erase and do over. I love to cut and paste. And besides, you can talk to a computer so you're never really alone.

* * *

I was back driving my Sunbeam Alpine, making the round trip from Casper to Laramie over good old Shirley Rim. I had plenty of time to think and numerous things to think about.

One thought that occupied my mind was the memory of finals in Whitewater. I was trying to figure out why the Anaheim Kingsmen's performance stood out so clearly in my memory. It was like they had broken through an invisible barrier between performer and observer: they invited me into their show. Their performance was totally alive and present.

It was spontaneous!

It shimmered magically, and sparkled continuously.

What made that possible? How did they do that?

It was the same mesmerizing sensation I had experienced in 1954 with Frankie Farr and the Appleknockers, and again with the Troopers in 1966 at the Gaelic Park show in the Bronx. It was becoming evident to me that the very best entertainers, those who consistently turn out spellbinding performances, must possess a ritualistic method of preparation, or some grand personal formula for success, or perhaps an extreme intention and need to communicate.

More things to think about.

Another thing that rattled around in my brain during those long lonely drives was, "What now?" I was going to graduate from college in just a couple of months and I had no idea what I was going to do. Other than the Troopers, I had no prospects for the future. I knew I wanted to teach, but the big question was did I want to teach in Casper, or go back out to California, or head east?

What I really wanted was to become the band director of Bergenfield High School, following in the footsteps of Dr. Baggs and Don Angelica, but Fred Sanford had already taken that position in September of '71, so it probably wouldn't be available any time soon.

Oh boy, I had a lot to think about.

* * *

Julian McClenahan was the music director at Kelly Walsh High School in Casper. He made student teaching an enjoyable experience for me. He was a fine musician, knowledgeable teacher, and good friend, and I don't know what I would have done if Julian hadn't been there when I needed help. He came through for me big time more than once.

As luck would have it, half way through the student teaching experience, the music director of a small oil town about 25 miles outside of Casper simply up and disappeared with the neighbor lady, or so the story went, and as it turned out the Natrona County Board Of Education was in need of a music director, pronto.

Being the only local prospect, I was immediately contacted by the superintendent. He proposed that he sign off on student teaching and several other little things for me, take care of moving expenses, and provide us with an apartment in the new teacher housing unit in Midwest. Along with all of this came the magic words…

Immediate money!

Real pay!

I hadn't received a steady paycheck since John was born. Just the thought of having a little extra cash was exhilarating. Edie and I celebrated immediately by purchasing a 1961 Mercedes Benz four door from the father of a lead soprano player in the corps. It was a fine automobile in great shape with leather upholstery, new tires, and plenty of warm wonderful heat. Just what the doctor ordered.

My graduation from the University of Wyoming was finalized in January 1973 thereby removing a tremendous weight from my shoulders. I was the first and only member of my family to have accomplished this feat of scholastic achievement and it felt good to have it done and over.

A few days later I received a phone call from Fred Sanford. He had decided that teaching high school band was not for him and he was wondering if I would be interested in applying for the position as band director for the Bergenfield band.

 Can you believe that?

Edie substituted for me at the Midwest High School so I could fly back east to interview for the position. I absolutely could not believe how things were turning out. To become the director of the Bergenfield band had been on my mind ever since Don Angelica invited me out to New Jersey to observe his setup at the school. That was back in 1966 when I was deciding whether or not to make the move out west to Wyoming.

I took the interview, they offered me the job, and I said yes.

I have to tell you that I was totally blown away. I was positive that no one else in the world knew of my desire to teach at Bergenfield. I had never told anyone. I simply focused on what I wanted and prepared for it the best I could.

Could it possibly be that is all one has to do?

* * *

During the summer of 1972 I'd had the opportunity to experience a Chicago Symphony performance at Ravinia, the outdoor concert hall in Highland Park. Sir George Solti was conducting Gustav Mahler's first symphony, *The Titan*. I was there with Jim Unrath, Don Angelica, and Fred Sanford.

From the opening note of the violins it was magical. I had never heard Mahler before. The music captured my mind. Nothing else existed but Mahler's music. I was completely alone, in a concert hall full of people. I think I was in rapture. Nothing like that has ever happened to me again.

While we were living in Midwest, Wyoming in the winter and spring of 1973, I studied Mahler's first symphony. I listened to it and read along with the score every day. It became a total obsession and it went on for weeks.

At that time my son John had been two years old.

Twenty-eight years later my son John called and said he had just heard a piece of music on the radio that he had never heard before, and that it was truly strange because he knew every single note of it. He was able to sing along with a piece of music that he had no memory of ever having heard. I asked him what piece of music he had been listening to and he said that it was Mahler's first symphony and that it was one of the weirdest experiences he had ever had.

The funny thing is that at the time John called to tell me his strange tale he was the exact same age that I had been all those years ago when I heard Mahler for the first time at Ravinia.

* * *

Teaching music in Midwest was one of those experiences that make you appreciate the little things in life. Our time there turned out to be a learning experience that I will never forget. It taught me that there are people in this world who do not see things even close to the same way I do.

Once again we packed up the family car. I had to sell my beautiful stereo to a fellow teacher in Midwest because there would be no room for it in the car on our trip across country.

When it finally came time to leave Casper in search of our new life on the east coast we chanced to drive directly under and through the most gigantic rainbow either of us had ever seen. There must have been a pot of gold on both ends holding it down.

East coast here we come!

* * *

It was a good year for the Troopers. We were nip and tuck all season with the Vanguard and finally placed second to them at the DCI final competition in Whitewater, Wisconsin.

Chapter 12
1974 Bergenfield and Muchachos

In a word, my experience at Bergenfield High School was intense. It was intense beyond imagination. For the first time in my life there were not enough hours in the day.

Life in Bergenfield was a huge change for Edie and me, especially considering where we had been living for the past six months. There were so many powerful personalities, and all of them seemed to be extending themselves out to us.

As the new band director I found myself completely surrounded by a full staff of people who knew exactly what to do and how to do it.

How great was that?

I wrote music and designed drill for the band proper, rehearsed and directed the full musical ensemble, and in general played the part of band director. Instruction of the all-girl color guard was left in the capable hands of Dennis and Mike Delucia. The percussion section was ably taken care of by Brian Callahan and George Vondeschmit. Don Angelica kept a close, but not too close eye on the band's activities from his lofty office in administration.

And then there was the man who made everything work, the man who always knew what had to be done next, the man who handled every situation like a consummate diplomat, Frank Levy.

Frank's number one responsibility was to keep yours truly on top of his responsibilities, and he did that amazingly well in addition to taking care of his own obligations and duties. I wish to thank you, Frank, for making it possible for me to be successful at what I do best.

Frank and I got along like Frick and Frack. We worked together, hung out together, and had deep conversations together, but from what

I remember most, we worked together. There were concerts, trips, competitions, field shows, festivals, parades, after school rehearsals, with the orchestra, with the marching band, the tenth grade band, and the concert band. It was a grueling schedule. I felt tremendous pressure to constantly produce at high levels of achievement.

The week after marching band season was over, Don Angelica called me to his office and congratulated me on the band's accomplishments. He also asked, as a personal favor to him, if I would add to my already busy schedule by taking on winter rehearsals with the Hawthorne Muchachos. I had no idea who the Muchachos were, except that they must have been in some way connected to the Hawthorne Caballeros.

I said I would be glad to do it but secretly felt that I was taking on too much, not only from the standpoint of time spent, but of having entirely too many things to think about, too many situations to consider, and not enough time to spend at home with Edie, John and Daphne on Closter Dock Road.

* * *

There was no doubt that I truly enjoyed teaching. Whether in the Bergenfield band room or the Muchachos' corps hall I was exactly where I belonged.

I enjoyed manipulating the learning environment from moment to moment, creating a proper rehearsal mood, staying aware that everyone remained present and accounted for physically, mentally, and psychologically.

As far as I was concerned, we were simply spending time to learn and improve, so that we could eventually blow ourselves away with moments of complete musical madness.

I loved to teach! And I was being given many opportunities to do so.

The Muchachos were very enjoyable to work with. What they truly excelled in was heart, the one thing you can't really teach. So I taught technique, tuning, and phrasing as an integral part of creating musical madness.

Toward the end of rehearsal Dennis Delucia's percussion section would come upstairs and put on a show for the brass, and believe me, they were hot!

What a hype! The brass section wanted desperately to return the favor, so they were always into whatever I came up with to help them "wow" the percussion.

But the biggest hype by far for the Muchachos brass section was Jeff Kievet. I didn't know anything about Jeff. Everybody said I wouldn't believe it when I heard him play and everybody was right. Jeff was an intense individual and played like he had been blessed by the god of brass mastery. It was an enormous treat just to hear him play.

* * *

On July 12th 1974 our second beautiful son was born to us.

Edie and I named him Timothy Michael.

When Timmy was only one month old, he accompanied Edie, brother John and myself to Ithaca, New York for the DCI World Championships.

Due to baby Tim's arrival in mid-July, and my having to teach summer music school at Bergenfield, I didn't have any time to tour with the Troopers, and since I had taught only the winter program for the Muchachos, I was completely free of drum corps responsibilities during DCI Championships. That meant that all four of us were going to the final show together for the first time ever.

And a great final show it was!

We arrived upstairs at our seats just before the Muchachos went on. I hadn't seen them perform since the first show of the year back in June. From the opening note of the dueling hornlines it was obvious to me that the east coast had a contender on the rise. The Muchachos broke the barrier that night just as Anaheim had done in '72. They connected with the audience big time. Jeff Keivet was the star of the night. As the old saying goes, "he had them eating out of the palm of his hand."

I had never heard or seen anything like it! The brass had a full hearted sound with full bore enthusiasm. The percussion rocked and cooked, and even the color guard attracted my eye a number of times, which is not easy because I mostly listen.

It was a stunning performance!

The Troopers were up next and they were playing new arrangements by Jim Ott, namely *Yankee Doodle Dandy, The Yellow Rose of Texas*, and *The Virginian*. They were fast, flashy, robust arrangements. Rumor had it that Jim Ott had to camp out on Mr. Jones' living room floor for a week to finish writing the show, then fly back to California where he arranged and taught for the Concord Blue Devils.

It was great to have the opportunity to appreciate the Troopers without the distraction of knowing every note and turn in the show. The Troopers performed up to their usual level of greatness that night.

The show moved on to the one and only Kilties from Racine, Wisconsin whose rousing *Brigadoon Fanfare* and *McDuffy's March* sent chills up my spine. I have always enjoyed hearing and seeing the Kilties perform, and I especially enjoyed when they so vividly recreated the sound and image of bagpipes in the mist, as they did that night.

Next corps on the starting line was the Santa Clara Vanguard. It was a classic Vanguard show with music from Wagner's Ring Cycle, Britten's *Young Person's Guide To The Orchestra*, Bernstein's Overture to *Candide*, and Steven Sondheim's *Send In The Clowns*, along with a slightly raucous rendition of the *Bottle Dance* from *Fiddler On The Roof* as an encore. The absolute standouts of the Vanguard's performance that night were Fred Sanford's musically powerful first place percussion and Pete Emmons' masterfully conceived blue ribbon visual design.

The 1974 Vanguard show and performance were something to savor and remember for years to come.

The next corps on the starting line was the Anaheim Kingsmen.

What an awesome display of talent, high energy, and musicianship. From the opening notes and rhythms of Bernstein's *Dance At The Gym* from West Side Story it was a tour de force of sound and visual effects. My most vivid memory was of Steve Beard's beautiful baritone solo in Stan Kenton's *Artistry In Rhythm*. Combine that with the bombastic qualities of Hector Berlioz's *Symphonie Fantastique*, and the smooth undulating harmonies of Tower of Power's *So Very Hard To Go* (complete with soprano solo to die for) and you have a show never to be forgotten.

All I could say was wow!

But the best brass was saved for last. 1974 was a breakthrough year for the Madison Scouts. Musical arrangements by Ray Baumgardt and brass instruction by Jim Elvord. The opening of the show, *Ballet In Brass*, was as lush and powerful as any brass lover could possibly ask. I was so glad for my exposure to Ray Baumgardt's methods. I could fully appreciate how that well stylized, powerful lightness was achieved. The quality of the brass had a certain transparency to it that I had never heard before. It was almost as though I could hear right through the sound. *God Bless The Child* and *Slaughter On Tenth Avenue* summed up one of the most enjoyable brass performance I had ever heard from a drum and bugle corps.

The Vanguard won the show that night with Madison second, Kingsmen third, Muchachos fourth and the Troopers fifth.

Chapter 13
Tuned to the Bone

Surprise, surprise, surprise! It was September 1974 and we weren't loading the family car up to go anywhere.

A guy could get used to this!

We were now residing in the town of Bergenfield, whereas we had been living about ten miles north and east, over by the Palisades. We were well situated in a three story duplex, not far from shopping and a short ride to school. The neighborhood was quiet and peaceful, except when a train went by. Trains went by like clockwork; freight trains, commuter trains, long trains, and short trains roared passed the back of our house only sixty feet or so from the kitchen window.

I found it amazing that I could become accustomed to such noise and vibration to the extent that I no longer gave it a thought.

My second year of teaching high school band was more productive than the first because I had a decent idea of what was coming next, and was therefore better able to plan for it.

I have a tendency to plan very slowly.

It is not what you might call methodical.

You might tag it as leisurely daydreaming.

At any rate, I was starting to get a good feel for what was coming next. Long before an event got to the planning stage I was beginning to make mental pictures of what I might like to see happen. That way, when it came time to take action, I had plenty of ideas floating around in my head. Nothing etched in stone, mind you, but lots of loose concepts from which to choose.

Speaking of loose concepts, one evening Frank Levy and I were sitting in his car chatting about this and that when Frank asked the question, "What is your impression of my impression of you?" to which I replied, "I don't understand the question," to which he replied, "What do you think I think of you?"

I was stumped!

I had no idea what Frank thought, and it would never have occurred to me to have an impression of what he thought of me. I told Frank that, and he told me I was weird. He said that most "normal" people walk around all the time with impressions in their heads of what others think of them.

I said, "You've got to be kidding me," but Frank went on to explain how many people live in worlds of unreality, worlds composed of incorrect impressions of how other people feel toward them, and that they then respond toward others based on these erroneous assumptions. He referred to this phenomenon as pigeonholing, which is like putting people into little mental cubbyholes, based on what you think they think of you, and further more, responding to them in ways which are based on how you feel about them, because of what you think they think of you.

Very confusing I know, but at the same time extremely enlightening… not to mention a little scary.

At the end of our little brain twister I turned to Frank and said, "So Frank, what is your impression of my impression of you," to which he gave me his signature expression of, wouldn't you like to know, (with a mischievous twinkle in his eye) and drove off.

* * *

Mike Benard was the choral director at Bergenfield High School. One evening in particular we had gotten together at his house to discuss the combined spring concert.

Mike had a frenetic way of speaking, which I found interesting, confusing, and fun. In a matter of moments he would quickly expound on a barrage of topics, and include his own considered opinions on each.

Then he would stop and wait... I could almost hear him mentally panting. He would just stare at me with a big smile frozen on his face, waiting for me to respond... And if I didn't respond quickly enough he would hit me with yet another volley of stuff.

So there we were, after everyone had left, just smoking and shooting the breeze. Mike was giving me his recipe for artichokes, which went something like this: So, you wash your artichokes and soak them in water for fifteen minutes or so. Then, cut off the stems at the base, and cut off the top third of the leaves. I prefer a serrated knife for this task.

Slice a lemon in half and smear one half, while squeezing it, all over the artichokes and fill the leaves with lemon juice. Boil them in enough water for them to float. Add salt, whole peppercorns, olive oil, the afore mentioned sliced lemon, and one smashed garlic clove to the water, cover and cook at a slow boil for forty-five minutes to an hour. When done, drain, sprinkle with rice wine vinegar and serve with a lemon mayonnaise dip.

Throughout this whole time Mike was bumming cigarettes from me because he had run out.

As I was about to leave Mike looked at me very seriously, slowed down his speech and said, "You're not really going to smoke around those beautiful little boys of yours, are you?"

His comment struck me like a freight train!

I saw in an instant how I had been hooked myself when I was only fourteen. My mother, my father and my brother all smoked.

I reached into my pocket, took out the package of cigarettes and tossed it over to Mike and said a sincere thank you and goodnight.

I didn't smoke, or think about cigarettes, for years after that evening.

* * *

One of my personal projects for the '74 '75 season was to check all of the school-owned brass instruments. I tested and checked each instrument for clarity of tone and tunability. I reamed mouthpiece ends and cleaned mouthpieces out.

One instrument in particular, a baritone horn, seemed especially uncared for. I took the mouthpiece out, reamed it, brushed it out and washed it out, put the mouthpiece in the horn, took a deep breath and attempted to play a tuning note. I heard the same muffled sound that the young man who uses this instrument makes when he tunes with the band.

First I checked to see if the valves were in correctly, but there was no problem there, so I put the water hose to it and lo and behold a green St. Patrick's Day bowtie came floating out the end of the bell.

I wonder how long that bowtie had been living in there.

It was truly amazing how much clearer the brass section sounded after my day of refurbishing, and the young man whose horn held the green bowtie wore a look of complete astonishment on his face during the tuning process. I did similar things with the woodwind instruments, checking reeds, tuning, general repair, and cleanliness.

One intonation activity that I particularly enjoyed was having a section of perhaps six or eight players gather around a full octave strobe and trade pitches down the line looking to match pitch with the strobe and match tones with each other. Once the players felt comfortable with matching a single pitch I would throw a simple two-count lick into the mix, which most of them would flub the first time around, but then they would get it and the tone matching would continue on until they all began to sound alike.

This was an ear training exercise. There was no music notation to interpret. The only visual stimulus was the little black spinning squares on the strobe, which told them if they were sharp, flat, or in-tune. Other than that it was strictly listening: listening and mimicking.

I have found that to create a professional sounding instrumental ensemble the performers must aspire to a professional level of intonation. Focused listening and resonant intonation are the cornerstones of fine ensemble performance.

Playing in an ensemble with exceptionally fine and stable intonation improves every performer's general level of self-confidence through supportive mutual resonance. Mutual resonance supports the very creation of sound, just as playing in a resonant chamber makes a player feel good and sound good.

If a wind instrument is tuned to agree with an ensemble's pitch and the performer plays in a well-focused manner, the resultant tone quality will be resonant with that of the ensemble.

If a wind instrument is tuned improperly, flat or sharp, and then "coerced" by the performer to play in-tune, a dissonant quality of sound will be set up within the instrument itself. The instrument's tone quality becomes compromised, due to the disagreement between the pitch indicated by instrument's improper tuning, and the performer's intention to play in-tune with the ensemble.

Mutual supportive resonance is achieved only when the ensemble's instruments are tuned properly (to a professional degree) and when the performers are focused intently on creating harmony and blend. The ability to create mutual supportive resonance consistently affords performers the opportunity to be at their best during rehearsals and performances. When the ensemble environment encourages performers to be at their best, the making of music becomes a much less complicated endeavor.

> "Music is simple enough. First the instruments are
> tuned. Then the piece is played to completion
> in harmony, the notes all clear, and without interruption."
> Confucius (to the Grand Maestro of Lu)

Here is a little story that came to me almost fully formed as a daydream. I could accomplish absolutely nothing else until it was all written down on paper.

Let us return to those primitive days of yesteryear, before the refinement of musicology, to see if we might call to mind some of those original feelings and sensations associated with the magical performance of music.

Tuned To The Bone

One day, Leonardo B. Ernstein was playing his favorite of all instruments, the flutabone, while seated in a lotus position outside of his cave. It was indeed a beautiful day and Leonardo was thoroughly enjoying the sounds of his instrument as they mixed with the cries of his pet pterodactyl.

Leonardo was the only musically minded man of the tribe, and although he had never taken lessons, he did feel that he could play his flutabone better than his pet pterodactyl could sing.

As Leonardo was about to cadence into the development section of his Fantasia on Fursleeves, he was interrupted by the sound of a stranger approaching. "I say stranger," cried Leonardo, "would you care for a bit of tea and conversation?"

The stranger was an extremely short, well muscled man, carrying a large sack over his shoulder. He replied to Leonardo, "Sure, I'd be glad to, if you can get that overgrown pelican to stop its awful moaning."

"Well," thought Leonardo, "let's see if this stranger is a man who understands true talent, or if he is perhaps just another would-be critic."

After dismissing his poor, dejected pet, Leonardo invited the stranger to come pull up a stone and sample some of his favorite herbal tea. The stranger said his name was Arondo Coplando and that he was traveling through the area with hopes of finding someone who might have similar interests in what he referred to as music.

To say the least, Leonardo and Arondo got along famously. Leonardo showed Arondo his flutabone, which he had painstakingly fashioned from a bone his wife had used to make her award-winning batch of triceratops and crops soup. This indeed pleased Arondo and he in turn showed Leonardo his instrument, which he removed from his large sack. It was a bonified bonafone that Arondo had purchased from a traveling salesman by the name of Vito Bonleone.

As you might imagine, Leonardo and Arondo lost no time at all in beginning their musical career. Day after day they could be seen roaming the hills, making beautiful music together.

One day Arondo said to Leonardo, "Why don't we go on a musical crusade and find others who would like to make music with us?" This sounded like a fine idea to Leonardo, so they went back to his cave and made ready for the trip.

Upon leaving, Leonardo kissed his wife goodbye and turned his pet pterodactyl loose, since he would no longer be there to keep him company. For two years, Leonardo and Arondo combed the countryside for fellow musicians, telling each of them to practice hard and to meet them on a certain date in the capital city of Sinfonia, where they would all band together in concert.

The long awaited day finally arrived. It was truly a beautiful day, and all of the musicians in their very best attire ready and eager to make music. Arondo stood up and addressed the assemblage.

"Fellow musicians, welcome, and thank you for coming and sharing this historic occasion with Leonardo and myself. For our first selection, Leonardo and I have composed a very special piece entitled Seventy Six Bonaphones, which we would now like to play for you."

So, Leonardo and Arondo performed their new composition so that the other musicians could hear and learn it. It was a stirring rendition and the musicians applauded wildly in appreciation of the fine music, which Arondo and Leonardo had composed. By now, many of the townspeople had begun to gather around to hear the new sounds of music.

At last the time had come for all of the musicians to play together and experience for themselves the wonderful sensations which Leonardo and Arondo had told them about. On cue, the musicians lifted their instruments to playing position and awaited Arondo's downbeat.

Well, as you might have guessed, the sound that broke the still morning air was not the beautiful sound that Leonardo and Arondo had hoped for. The townsfolk who had gathered around began yelling in disapproval. Poor Leonardo and Arondo looked at each other in disbelief. They had no idea what had gone wrong. They were quite sure that each of the musicians could play beautifully, for they had auditioned each and every one personally.

After things had subsided, a little old man approached the musicians and said, "Pardon me, but uh, why don't you tune them bones?" Obviously, Leonardo and Arondo hadn't a clue as to what the man meant, so they asked him to introduce himself and explain what he could possibly mean by tune them bones.

"J.C. Strobabone at your service," the man said, "and I can tell you that the length of the bone is directly proportioned to the pitch of the tone."

"Well," said Leonardo, "I don't think I understand quite what you mean by the length of the pitch and the tone of the bone, or is it the tone of the pitch and the length of the bone?"

"Doesn't matter!" replied J. C. "Organization, that's what it's all about… Organization!"

"Do you mean that we have to organize the sound of our ensemble by adjusting the length of the bones?" asked Arondo.

"Give that man a cigar!" exclaimed J.C. "I think he's got it!"

Almost as if it had been rehearsed, the musicians broke into song (to the tune of "The Rain in Spain Stays Mainly on the Plain")

The length of bone determines the pitch of tone (J.C. *"I think they've got it"*) *The length of bone determines the pitch of tone… cha cha cha!"*

This was all well and good, but Leonardo had just one question, "Tell me, J.C. if we adjust these bones like you say, will we then be able to enjoy our music with a group as large as this?"

"My good man, I would stake your life on it." J.C. replied.

So they all got to work and, with J.C.'s help, they were able to adjust all of the instruments so that the short bones were all the same length and, therefore, had the same pitch: and the large bones matched exactly, only an octave lower.

J.C. was especially busy, for he had to check every instrument to see that it measured up to standards. He would play a bonafone and then tell the musician to "shave a quarter inch off the femur, and take a shade off the top of the third hole." He was often heard chanting over and over, "Bore it and hone it and measure the bone, and don't forget to check the tone; make them all play without a hitch, and don't forget to check the pitch."

And so it was that all of the men worked long and hard until at last their work was done and they could try once again to make music together.

The next morning the musicians all gathered in the huge courtyard.

Before they began however, J.C. told them, "Now that all of the bones are tuned, all you have to do is listen closely to the sounds around you as you play. By doing this, you can organize the sound as much as you like."

Just at that moment, Leonardo and Arondo began playing their composition and, to the musicians, their sounds were like the singing of angels. One by one, the musicians added in their own sounds and, little by little the sound of the group became larger and even more beautiful. People again began to gather together from all around to hear the new sound, only this time, they applauded very enthusiastically, for none of them had ever heard anything like it before. Why, even the musicians stood and applauded, for they had finally experienced for themselves the exhilaration and joy of making music with others.

The End

Chapter 14
1975 Bergenfield and Muchachos

Shortly after the winter break of 1975, Don Angelica called me to his office to congratulate me on the band's performance during the holiday concert, and asked me, as a personal favor to him, to spend some time working with a little corps near Pittsburgh, Pennsylvania by the name of the Fineleyville Royal Crusaders. He thought they had a chance of making finals that year and he just wanted to give them an extra boost. Of course, my reply was, I would be happy to.

But to tell the truth, I was finding that the lifestyle I was leading was not the lifestyle I was looking for. Perhaps a single man would have felt that this was a great way of life, but as a husband, father, and man of the world, it seemed an all consuming proposition to me. It was demanding more than I wished to give, and I believe Edie was feeling similarly. She was missing her mom and I think we both missed the wide open spaces of Wyoming and California. The environmental difference between the east coast and west coast is vast and I guess once you've developed a passion for one or the other, you feel slightly out of place anywhere else.

* * *

In the late evening of Easter Sunday 1975 a strange thing happened to me. I was watching T.V. and a program came on by the name of Yoga For Health. The man, who appeared to be a yogi, spoke at a wonderfully slow pace and seemed to be speaking directly to me. His name was Richard Hittleman. He and his female associate would take the viewers through a series of yoga poses at a nice easy pace, along with full explanation and information as to proper breathing and mental pose.

I sat through the whole program that night, didn't move a muscle. I wasn't even tempted to get down on the floor. I was quite content to just sit, watch, and listen. Yoga in 1975 America was not the rage it is today. If you did yoga back then, you were considered strange. So I just sat and watched the show that night, and the next night, and then night after night at 11:00 for the rest of that week.

After a week of sitting and watching Richard Hittleman, along with his associate, perform yoga poses, I found myself down on the floor doing the yoga movements I had been soaking up mentally every night that week. To say the least, I found the experience of performing the asanas (postures) refreshing.

I felt my perspective change during the program. My mind was actively operating my body while listening to Richard Hittleman speak. It was a similar experience to that of controlling a musical instrument while playing along with a music minus one tape; the one great exception being that in yoga there is no foreign device being manipulated, just the mind and body moving together from one moment to the next at the casual speed of real time.

And that was the difference!

That was what had caused me to sense a change in my perception. My mind had slowed down to the speed of reality, which is where my body lives all the time.

The body lives in real time

It resides in the here and now

It reproduces the species and lives by the sweat of its brow

The human mind on the other hand

Is free to roam and wander

Speed up, slow down, or repeat

Stop, create, or ponder

It was like suddenly discovering that your car indeed had a brake pedal!

It was possible to "stop the world" if you wanted to!

Needless to say, I became a yoga freak. I purchased Richard Hittleman's book, Twenty Eight Days To Yoga, and set aside time each day to gain better control over my body and mind. After practicing diligently day after day for about a week, a sense of serenity crept slowly into my life. Not so much as anyone would notice, but things began to slow down just a bit. It was nice to be able to exhibit some degree of control and understanding where my body and mind were concerned.

Learn to clear your mind

As you might clear your desk

Take care of that which won't wait

Place everything else in its proper state

Put it away for another day

Once your mind is clear of these things

It is time to sit quietly and wait

To see what concoction your mind will wrought

To intrude on your peaceful state

Spend some time in quiet mode

Illuminate internal awareness

Live in the moment in the land of you

Where there are many things for you to do

If thoughts come by your internal eye

Just watch

Don't get involved

Let them glitter and flitter away

Fizzle like clouds on a sunny day

* * *

The Muchachos' fourth-place finish at DCI the past season had brought in many fine players to audition. The addition of these talented performers made it possible to get more done during our weekly rehearsals. Considering where the brass ensemble had started a year ago, I was very pleased with its progress.

Working with the Muchachos in 1975 was a thrill. Electricity filled the air at every rehearsal. I had experienced that same sense of purpose and achievement during rehearsals with the Skyliners, the Troopers, and the Vanguard, but never with the Air Force Corps. The Air Force was not a competitive unit. There was no pot of gold to be sought, no defining moment to achieve.

It felt as though huge quantities of energy were being specifically attracted toward our particular place in the universe. It may have only been a Friday night rehearsal but the performers were looking forward to that spine-tingling thrill of playing with the hottest drum corps on the east coast. They wanted to know first hand the exhilaration of performing with the sound and emotion that had brought the fans of Ithaca, New York to their frenzied feet throbbing in unison "East! East! East! East!" Those members of the Muchachos who had witnessed the overwhelming explosion of humanity on that Saturday night in Ithaca will never forget the experience, the joy, the excitement, the intensity of the moment, and the thrill of a lifetime.

We are entities of energy connected through an ocean of energy in motion
Which undulates and stirs with the movement of the stars
And sends its mighty currents across the universe to Mars
Energy in motion throughout the vast celestial ocean
Surging with the origins of creation
Through canyons and cities over oceans and land
The power of the cosmos is there in your hand
Avail yourself of these energy streams
Use the force to build your dreams

* * *

Toward the end of spring semester that year the word came down from on high that the board of education would not be issuing contracts to non-tenured teachers due to budget problems. Even though I had been assured by one and all that I had nothing to worry about as far as my job was concerned, Edie and I decided after long deliberation that it was time for us to head back out west.

So at the end of the school year we once again loaded up the Mercedes, this time with a U-haul carrier attached to the top, and began the trek home to Wyoming. We stopped off in Fineleyville, Pennsylvania where we all stayed for a few days in a mobile home on the Monongahela River, while I spent some time working with the Royal Crusaders.

As we drove further west I found myself wrestling with a distant but nagging thought, which basically translated as, "What now?" "Where do I go from here?" "Is it over, am I done now?"

I didn't have any answers at the time, but I knew very well that when I left New York City back in 1967 I was going on a long adventure, and that in an adventure you never know what's coming next. So I put the whole thought package on the back burner and let it simmer. I wasn't going to worry about the future until I had delivered my family safely to Yia Yia's doorstep.

* * *

I went along on nationals tour with the Troopers, who were not up to their usual best. It looked as though the show had been put together at the last minute and the performers were still trying to mentally form the pieces into a cohesive whole.

To my ear, the Madison Scouts were the corps to beat at the DCI World Competition that year, especially due to the fact that the Muchachos had been disqualified from final competition.

Madison had been moving steadily upward since 1973 when Jim Elvord took over the brass program and instituted new show design concepts for the Scouts. He and Ray Baumgart had given them a whole new image and sound. But more importantly, Jim gave the performers both the right and the tools to perform their hearts out. And in my book, nothing beats that.

The Troopers took twelfth place in the preliminary competition and would have been out of the final show if the Muchachos had not been disqualified. The Fineleyville Royal Crusaders placed seventh in prelims and ninth at finals.

The Madison Scouts won the show. Their hornline set new standards in both the general effect and technique areas of performance, and, they set new standards for the ultimate hornline I one day hoped to create.

Chapter 15
1976 Troopers

In September of 1975 Mr. Jones once again made me an offer I couldn't refuse. He said that he needed to spend more time with his business. There were a few large projects he wanted to develop in Casper, starting with a retirement home to be named after his second daughter Laurel. He said that he would like me to take over the day-to-day responsibilities of directing the corps. For my services he offered a salary and a substantial loan for Edie and me to buy a house in Casper and settle down.

I guess that answered the nagging question of "what now?"

I had no other prospects for the immediate future, and I had no idea of what I was getting myself into by accepting the position as Trooper director, but as was my custom I said I would check with Edie and that barring any unforeseen problems I'd be glad to do it.

We found a house that we both fell in love with, not far from where Edie's mom lived.

We settled down.

John was four and Timmy was fifteen months. We had plenty of time for family, hobbies, and mini vacations in Thermopolis, Wyoming. Thermopolis is a hot springs resort about two hours northwest of Casper and the drive to Thermopolis through the Wind River Canyon is one of the most beautiful I have ever experienced.

Life was good!

After having been on the go for so many years here we were, the four of us, alive and well and living in our own home in Casper, Wyoming.

Who would have thought?

To be at home, to be at ease... Home safe and secure
To be there, in the lair, where it's always okay
Where no one will say anything to dismay
Where respect for one another
Father, sister, mother, brother
Is the basis for allowing each to live a life unique
Where one can be.....without pressure
Live..... at one's leisure
Deadlines are rubberized and no one is patronized
Everyone's free to be, be, and be
To become and proceed through thought word and deed
A place like no other!
A haven!
A safe zone!
Believe me when I say there should be
No Place Like Home

* * *

While living in Bergenfield, New Jersey, I had acquired a new, blue, Schwinn ten-speed bicycle with a child's seat attached to the back. The seat was situated directly behind my own. John learned quickly to sit up straight and not lean too far into the turns. John and I spent many wonderful hours racing all over Bergen County.

Upon arriving back in Casper we found that John had grown too big for the back seat of my bicycle, so we purchased a bike for John and a bike for Edie. Off we would go, with Timmy in tow on the back seat of my blue bike, with Edie riding point, not allowing anyone to slip by, and John pedaling fast enough to make a good try, down the hill and over the rise to Yia Yia's house.

Or up the hill, slow and steep, then a right-turn onto McKinley Street. "Watch out for cars," we all warned and barked, then a zig and a zag down to Washington Park.

I tried taking Daphne the Great Dane on bike rides but she just never took to it, at least not like she took to riding in the Sunbeam with the top down, and the wind blowing through her long elegant ears. She would sit straight up in the passenger seat next to me, wallowing in the adoration coming from everyone who saw her. She would just look at me with her ears blown straight up in the air as though to say, "What do you think? Am I hot or what?"

* * *

I was very surprised to discover that Fred Sanford had taken over the position of corps director with the Madison Scouts. I had the feeling that Fred and I were on parallel paths somehow, and that we had been ever since our first meeting at Mr. Jones' house in 1967. Fred and I had become good friends, the only problem being that we were seldom in the same place at the same time. But when we did get together, there was always a party!

Fred loved to party!

* * *

I found out soon enough that being the director of a drum and bugle corps was not really up my alley. It was not what I had spent my whole life preparing for. I had no expertise. I was a brass instructor, a teacher, a player, but once again I was put in the position of being the arranger and director, spending many hours sitting down with pencil and paper... and you know how I feel about that.

I experienced two wonderful drum corps moments during the 1976 season. We had scheduled the Troopers for a trip to Canada for the Calgary Stampede and Rodeo in early July. My son John was five years old, old enough to take care of himself, so he came along with us in the staff car, which was a new, donated, pea green station wagon. The staff car acted as an overflow valve for staff members and corps members alike, and became the change of scenery from the inside of a bus!

So my son John got to know everyone in the corps and everyone got to know John.

Along with the mixture of folks who came to ride with us in the staff car there also came a variety of music. Everyone brought his or her favorite tapes to play and listen to as we traveled. John and I were inundated with styles and textures of music. John's favorite song that week was Paul Simon's *Fifty Ways To Leave Your Lover*. And his favorite line was "you don't need to discuss much," which came right after the line "just hop on the bus, Gus." The melody was more than a little out of John's range but that was what made it so cute.

The Troopers were the hit of the Stampede show. They performed in conjunction with the Young Canadians who were truly wonderful. The Young Canadians presented scenes from *A Chorus Line* complete with mirrors, dancing, and song, and were accompanied by a fine show band. The Troopers performed their full musical show with a somewhat altered drill, and they did it on a stage that was huge, although not quite large enough to accommodate a full drum corps show.

During the final night of the Stampede it began to rain, it began to rain hard, but to the absolute delight of the audience, who were covered by a giant overhang, the Troopers turned on the performance of the year. It was one of those electric moments when both the performers and audience lose themselves in a back and forth feeding frenzy. It was an evening never to be forgotten.

The second most memorable moment of the 1976 season was seeing and hearing the Blue Devils perform. My first viewing of them was in Denver. They were wearing light blue, short sleeve shirts, if I remember correctly, because their new uniforms had not yet come in. Something about the Blue Devils resonated deep within me.

I loved the sound of their hornline!

I loved the choice of music!

And the North drums were totally outrageous!

There was something about the total package that emitted a sense of power and strength. They were very well presented. They were strong in every caption, but especially they were strong in brass. The arrangements were by Jim Ott. I had met Jim back in the late sixties while I was attending San Jose State and instructing the Santa Clara Vanguard. Jim had been teaching and arranging for the Stockton Commodores and he asked me to come down and give a brass clinic to the hornline. It was at that clinic that I met Jim's talented and lovely sister, Bonnie Ott, who could blow the bell off a mellophone with the sweetest tone you ever heard.

So now, here was Jim Ott wielding one of the hottest hornlines I had ever heard and his sister Bonnie was the "to die for" mellophone soloist.

You guessed it! I was hyped!

Their final performance at DCI was the clincher. The Blue Devils were a force to be reckoned with.

* * *

Both Fred and I had taken our respective drum corps one step down the ladder from the year before. Fred had taken the Scouts from first to second place at finals and I had gone from twelfth to thirteenth place with the Troopers.

By the time I returned home from DCI my mind was in an uproar. The year had been a total disaster for me personally. There was one thing I knew for certain; I wanted nothing to do with drum corps.

Chapter 16
1977 SPEBSQA and Wooden Toys

As foretold in Chapter 7 of this volume my internal world finally collapsed, and enveloped me in a darkness I would never have believed existed. I was a ship without a rudder or even a destination to paddle toward. I had no idea what was going on.

Had I had lost my mind?

There was no doubt that I had lost my way.

The world was no longer my oyster. It held no interest for me.

I was lost in a world of my mind.

Complete and utter chaos raged between my ears. I didn't have a clue as to what had happened or what could be done about it, but I knew on some level that no one was going to be able to help. How could anyone possibly help if I didn't know what was wrong myself? I suppose I could have gone into analysis. That would have been one way of dealing with the problem, but I had always been a do it myself kind of guy, so it was up to me to find a way out of the deep, dark, hole I had somehow stumbled into.

Survival instinct kicked in. I had a wife and two little boys to support.

I had to get a job!

A job doing what?

I wanted nothing to do with drum corps or band.

So I got a job at a glass shop, in downtown Casper, where I learned to break glass. That wasn't what they were trying to teach me, but that was what ended up happening. I eventually figured out how to get the glass to break the way I wanted it to break.

From there on it became fun.

The first thing I did with my new found talent was to build an all glass pyramidal planter for the living room. It was about two feet square by two feet high and housed a few of my favorite coleus plants.

I think Edie liked it but I couldn't tell for sure.

This was the first time I had ever worked in the field of fabrication and I was intrigued by the possibilities. I began to work with wood.

The garage was cold but it was a place to work. I put a little shop together. Edie's brother Marv, who was working at the time as a carpenter, helped me with the building of my workbench. Edie and I went to garage sales for a couple of weekends to find the tools I needed. With those few tools and a small stack of hand picked lumber I was ready to go. That is, all except for the books. Of course I had to research woodworking just as I had researched Socrates, yoga, photography, education, and acoustics.

Thank you, Mr. Hanselman!

In September of 1976 Edie embarked on her career as a banker. Thirty years down the road she would have worked practically every aspect of banking and won every award there is to be won. But in September of 1976 she took a job as teller in the First Wyoming National Bank of Casper.

So now Edie and I were both working. John was almost six years old and attending elementary school just one block east of our house. Timmy was two, not terrible two, just plain two, and attending the Kid Korral located a few blocks from where both Edie and I worked. Daphne the Great Dane was the only one at home during the day.

We were living the nine to five existence. If nothing else, it was predictable and routine.

* * *

It finally became obvious to me that I was in a deep state of depression. Knowing that I was depressed didn't really change anything, but it was better than being completely in the dark. I also came to understand that I had lost all sense of direction in relation to my future endeavors as a man of the world. That is to say, how I would use my talents, how I would be creative, and how I would live by my father's singular advice, "find something you love to do and do it."

It didn't take me long to figure out that I didn't want to work in a glass shop for the rest of my life, but I did discover that I enjoyed using tools to produce new and different creations. Over the next fifteen months I created hand carved jewelry boxes for family members and two hand carved toy chests for John and Tim. Both toy chests were entered at the Central Wyoming Fair and both received the blue ribbon in their respective class.

Oh boy!

I also started a wooden toy business. We called it Wood 'n Things. Pretty original, huh? By Christmas of 1978, an artist friend and I had designed, created, and sold, scores of hand painted wooden puzzles, biplanes, tanks, animal puzzles, hand carved photo albums, and my favorite, adorable little rocking cradles.

Designing and creating both of the boys' toy chests took hundreds of hours of work, and it was time spent all alone. Carving a sailing ship on a wooden ocean complete with searching seagulls takes a very fine concentration, the kind of concentration that requires the mind to slow down to carving speed.

I recall that it would sometimes take as long as an hour for the speed of my mind to match the movements of my hands. Sometimes it never did synchronize completely, and when it didn't, I paid the price in mistakes and screw-ups.

But eventually, when I sat down to carve, my mind would synchronize quickly, as a matter of course. That is, if I wasn't in the middle of a mental hailstorm. I had learned the importance of calming myself before going into action, and I found that I could only accomplish this by incorporating an extremely vigilant style of awareness.

* * *

Awareness is a most interesting commodity, for in the wilds of nature, a lack of environmental awareness can mean swift and sudden death! Awareness is the access key to all knowledge! Awareness constitutes your ability to see what is real and true within you, about you, above you, and below you. Awareness is the only tool you have to tame the undisciplined beast of a brain inside your head. Through full time awareness life can become clear. Through awareness the inner you can become healthy. Awareness is paying close attention to all of your senses in a passive yet investigative way, almost primitive. Lightly tethered to the world of the thinking mind the true wonder of life is revealed through our purest experiences. We are enriched by the memories and understanding they bring.

* * *

In September of 1976 I was contacted on behalf of a chapter of the Society for the Preservation and Encouragement of Barbershop Quartet Singing in America.

They wanted me to be their director!

They had been referred to me by Gordon Sanford, Fred Sanford's dad. I soon found out that Mr. Sanford was a barbershopper. He sang baritone.

I was now an official barbershop chorus director, and I loved it. In August of 1977 the chapter sent me to St. Joe, Missouri to attend the SPEBSQA Harmony College, a one-week marathon of singing, carousing, and learning.

I had the opportunity to sing with a bass section composed of over one hundred men, in an auditorium jam-packed with over four hundred men. The director of this giant quartet was an extraordinary personality who appeared suddenly upon the stage; his every word, movement, and gesture suggested musicality, expression, and precision.

During classes held throughout the week we learned about vocal music from many points of view: sound production, breathing, science of intonation (right up my alley), psychology of singing, rehearsal and show strategies, conducting techniques, and a short, hands-on seminar based on the joys of quartet singing while drinking an ice cold beer.

Harmony College was the single most intense week of musical learning and male bonding I had ever experienced, and it went a long way towards setting me straight again as far as my bouts of depression went.

This was the first time in over ten years that I had not attended the drum corps championships in August. As a matter of fact, the only drum corps show I had seen in 1977 was in late July. The only reason I went to the show was that it was held in Casper and I wanted to see the Blue Devils again. Unfortunately, I found the Blue Devils' show and performance disappointing. The word going around the stands was that the corps members had become ill while practicing and performing in Utah and were just beginning to recover from it.

Chapter 17
1978 27th Lancers

In September of 1977 I was spending most of my time out in the garage with Daphne the Great Dane, cutting, drilling, shaping and sanding. 'Wood 'n Things' was in full swing and I was jazzed. Larry McCormick had given me an order for twenty-five wooden clocks that he wished to give out as Christmas presents.

While working on my 'Wood 'n Things' projects I was doing some research into the mechanics of acoustics. In general, I was interested in the acoustical properties of resonators, but in particular I was zeroing in on closed and open pipes (resonators) and how they affect their intrinsic vibrating systems.

All musical instruments are composed of at least one generator and one resonator.

Resonators support and amplify the vibrations of generators. Some resonators, like the soundboard of a piano or the soundbox of a guitar, will support and amplify all of the many tones and pitches created by the vibrating strings of the instrument.

Other resonators, like the closed pipe of a reed organ or the resonating tubes below the bars of a marimba, will support and amplify only one pitch.

I was interested in the fact that the closed pipe of a reed organ not only supported and amplified the sound produced by its generator (the vibrating reed) it also dominated the pitch of the reed. That is to say that the reed had no choice but to vibrate the pitch that corresponded to the length of the closed pipe.

With that said, I wanted to know how the bugle (resonator #1) in combination with the oral/thoracic cavity (resonator #2) affected the quality of vibration produced by the generator (performer's lips).

My thought was that if the two resonators were set to agree precisely on the pitch to be played, then the lips would receive a clear signal to vibrate that certain pitch. If, however, the two resonators were not in agreement, the lips would receive an ambiguous signal, creating dissonance within the vibrating system, thereby distorting the sound produced. Hmmmm!

While I was struggling with my resonator research, I was also attempting to build a machine that would accurately measure the precise length of a brass instrument. The idea was to generate a waveform in the instrument by using a mechanical generator to create the vibration, and a decibel meter to record the volume of the sound produced. By moving the tuning slide of the instrument in or out, the decibel meter would indicate the highest reading when the instrument's length agreed exactly with the pitch being produced by the mechanical generator… I think!

You can see that my mind was becoming healthier. As long as I kept it engaged with search and discover activities it stayed pretty much positive and upbeat.

* * *

Word that I had attended the Harmony College filtered through the barbershop community and I lucked out with the opportunity to coach several quartets, one of which was a Sweet Adeline Quartet. Sweet Adelines are female barbershoppers, and all of the women involved in the quartet had kids or grand kids who were desperately in need of wooden toys for Christmas.

I was networking!

I used the suggestions that were given during the Show Seminar at Harmony College to put our Christmas Barbershop Extravaganza together, and if I do say so myself it was a beauty. The highlight of the show was the full chorus singing *Paddlin' Madeline Home*, while an old fashion bathtub on wheels was pulled slowly across the stage on a rope. Inside of the tub sat my seven-year-old son John, along with the granddaughter of one of the men in the chorus. John was dutifully rowing away while the young lady sitting across from him in the tub batted her eyes at John and everyone else in the auditorium. She took her part very seriously.

The bathtub scene would have been John's debut performance if it weren't for the fact that he had just played his first piano recital two weeks earlier. As you can imagine, we were very proud parents. Seeing my son up on the stage about to give his first piano recital put a smile so big on my face it almost hurt. He was playing a tune by the name of *Bubble Gum Rhapsody* and he was dressed in a light blue suit that we had purchased specifically for the performance.

So there we sat, Edie and me in the front row, looking up at John as he prepared to play. I was amazed at how easily he seemed to be handling the situation. He had the selection memorized so there was no need to set up his music. His teacher introduced him, he sat down, adjusted his seat, and off he went.

All went well until he got about half way through the piece at which point he froze. He just stopped cold. I had no idea what had happened. He looked down at me with a look that said, "Dad, please help me!" but I just sat there, with the same big proud papa smile plastered across my face looking like everything was just fine. I decided to keep the smile because I thought it would be better than a frown or a scowl, and besides, I had no idea what else to do.

John rolled his eyes at me and slumped his shoulders as if to say, "A lot of help you are," then turned back to the piano and began the piece again from the beginning. This time he played straight through the tune without mishap and received a big hand from the gathered assemblage, not only for his fine piano playing, but also for heroically avoiding an uncomfortable scene.

* * *

About a week before Christmas 1977 I received a phone call from Jim Elvord. He was calling to ask if I would consider working with the 27th Lancers of Revere, Massachusetts. He said that he had worked the previous year with them but was unable to do so for the '78 season. I told him that I would have to think about it. He gave me George Bonfiglio's phone number (George was the director of the Lancers) and told me how much he would appreciate my help in the matter.

Edie and I discussed the possibilities at length. I hadn't actually taken on the responsibility of working a hornline for a whole season since I had taught the Troopers in 1973, but Edie said she had complete faith in me, so I decided to try it out.

I knew right away that I had made the right decision. The Lancers' staff was made up of some of the nicest people I had ever met, and practically everyone on that staff eventually made it into the DCI Hall of Fame.

The most fascinating person of all was George Zingali. George's mind was faster, funnier, and more creative than any I had ever come in contact with. George was a storm of activity and you never knew what he would say or do next. He was a wonder, an inspiration, and an absolute genius. I will always miss him.

I spent one week out of each month from January through May in Revere at the home of Charlie and Patty Poole. Charlie was the percussion instructor for the Lancers and his wife Patty enjoyed telling George B. (Bonfiglio) how things needed to be done. Patty and Charlie treated me like a guest, a king, and a family member all at the same time. We would sit up nights after rehearsals or after staff meetings (which were always held at the local bar) talking, kibitzing, drinking beer, and smoking cigarettes. Charlie and Patty both smoked like chimneys, and if you recall, I had quit smoking back in '74 when my son Tim was born. But I could not withstand the onslaught of billowing smoke night after night without indulging a little. I don't think I'd ever had more fun just sitting around and talking as I did those evenings at Charlie and Patty Poole's house.

On one evening in particular I had the opportunity to work on Charlie's hands. My idea was to see if I could change the tension level in the muscles of Charlie's arms by using traction on his wrists, hands, and fingers. The session lasted close to forty-five minutes, but by the end Charlie's hands felt soft and pliable, and exhibited a healthy sense of elasticity from elbow to fingertips. Charlie, being a percussionist, possessed an excellent sense of the tension levels in his arms and hands. He said after the session that his hands felt lighter than he could ever remember. He picked up a pair of drumsticks and his hands flew through a lick or two. Charlie was quite impressed, as was I.

That was the first time I had ever used that technique; as a matter of fact, that was the first time I had ever done anything like that with anyone.

From that point in time onward people were always willing to give me a hand, or a foot, in order to receive a session of what they referred to as "being pulled." It was fascinating to get to know people in this touch-oriented way, and believe me, everyone was different, especially in the area of elasticity. I guess I had been lucky to begin this work with Charlie Poole because Charlie was basically a relaxed kind of guy. With others, it was a longer, more involved process to obtain similar results.

Very interesting!

* * *

During the early part of 1978 I happened to read an article about Jerry Seawright and the Blue Devils. More to the point, it was an interview with Jerry Seawright about his involvement with the Blue Devils. Everything Jerry said supported my idea of the environment necessary for people to be successful and to accomplish their dreams. He expected his staff to be the best, but not without his full support.

As the season wore on I became more and more certain that I would one day work with the Blue Devils. I even told the Lancers' staff that I would be teaching the Blue Devils in 1979, but in truth I had told no one else, except Edie. Keep in mind, however, that I was beginning to believe whole heartedly in the premise that if you are dedicated to your dreams and you work hard to be fully prepared, then your dreams will come to you.

A very wise man put the concept this way:

"Your success in life does not altogether depend on your ability and training; it also depends on your determination to grasp opportunities that are presented to you. Opportunities in life come by creation not chance.

"It is not your passing inspirations or brilliant ideas so much as your everyday mental habits that control your life. Habits of thought are mental magnets that draw to you certain things, people, and conditions.

"If you learn to withdraw your attention from all objects of distraction and to place it on one object of concentration, you too will know how to attract at will whatever you need."

Paramahansa Yogananda

* * *

In late June of 1978 we loaded our new Datsun F10 Wagon and headed east to Chicago.

John, Tim, and I were off on our first adventure alone, without Edie, who had decided to stay home to keep watch on a not so perky Great Dane.

John was 7 years old, Tim was 3 years old, and as Edie put it, I should have been old enough to know better.

We were heading down the road to spend an evening in Chicago with Larry and Joy McCormick and to meet up with George Zingali, who was flying into Chicago to meet up with us. From there, our destination would be Myrtle Beach, South Carolina, to join up with the Lancers for their east coast tour.

We started our five thousand mile male bonding trip by traveling south out of Casper on Interstate 25 toward Douglas. From there we took highway 20, a narrow, two lane strip of blacktop that wound its way ever so slowly through the green rolling hills of Nebraska.

The boys were fun to be with. They loved to play games and they were good at them. One of our favorites was a math game that we had started playing on one of our trips to Thermopolis. I would give a math problem and it was up to them to figure out the answer. I always started with easy addition questions like "one plus one is?" to which the answer would come loud and clear, "two." My questions would become more and more difficult until the boy's responses became non-existent. At that point I would start with easy subtraction problems until they became too difficult and then on to multiplication and division. Mostly, they would come up with the right answers, but when they miscalculated I simply moved on to the next question.

I felt that this was a game not a test, a game to stimulate mathematical thinking in a fun supportive atmosphere, so I eliminated the negative aspect of being wrong and wholeheartedly supported the idea of full participation.

Another game that we all enjoyed was a game of opposites, which John and I had created one day while jumping up and down on a bed. It went something like this: I would sing, What's the opposite of up? (To a little melody that had materialized out of nowhere), and the answer would come, Down. What's the opposite of in? Out. What's the opposite of over? Under. What's the opposite of wet? Dry.

As you can see, this game could go on forever, but the first time John and I played it, John came up with the perfect ending. We had been playing for quite some time and I guess John was tired of jumping up and down, so when I asked the question, What's the opposite of high? John grabbed the opportunity to end it by jumping down from the bed and crying out "Goodbye" as he sailed out the door.

Our five thousand mile trip lasted a little over two weeks. It was truly an experience of a lifetime. John and Tim were introduced to hundreds of people they had never met before and by the end of our stay with the Lancers they knew many of them by name.

Memories of Larry McCormick sitting on the floor with three- year-old Tim playing smash up derby, George Bonfiglio barbecuing burgers for one hundred and fifty hungry folks, George Zingali, John, and Tim frolicking in the warm sands of Myrtle Beach, and having to say goodbye to one and all when we reached Boston, are etched in the fabric of our beings. I sometimes wonder how different life would be if opportunities like these had never come to be.

How far does five thousand miles of spontaneous, serendipitous life take you?

* * *

By the end of the 1978 season the Lancers had improved beyond belief. Jim Wedge, long time Lancer brass instructor, who had been absent from the corps for a while, came back to teaching during the summer of '78 and replaced a failing concert production with *"Celebrate,"* a tune the corps had used to great effect in 1975. They placed ninth in prelims and seventh in finals.

The top three spots in the DCI preliminary competition were garnered by Phantom Regiment in first, the Vanguard in second, and the Blue Devils in third. The three corps were separated by a mere five tenths of a point. In the DCI final competition first place was awarded to the Vanguard, second place to Phantom Regiment, and third place to the Blue Devils.

The interesting thing about placement in the brass caption that night was that Jim Ott, who had won high brass awards as caption head of the Blue Devils in 1976 and 1977, had gone over to Spirit of Atlanta for the 1978 season, and managed to walk off with the high brass award once again with a corps that had placed twenty-third overall the year before.

That was the talent of Jim Ott.

Jim was nothing short of amazing!

After the show that evening, Edie, John, Tim, and myself happened to find the new brass caption head of the Blue Devils leaning up against the back fender of our little blue Datsun F10.

I had no idea how he had picked my car out of the twenty thousand or so cars in Mile High Stadium, and neither did he. He was as surprised as I was, and was obviously upset about something, so I said, "Hey dude, what's the problem?" He dabbed at his eyes and mumbled something about losing the competition. So I took the opportunity to say, "What you need is me on your brass staff," to which he replied, "Would you really consider doing that?" to which I said, with a slight hesitation as I checked with Edie, "Sure, sign me up!" We exchanged phone numbers and he said he would check it out with Jerry Seawright and the rest of the staff and get back to me in a few days.

And that was that. How's that for karma?

I received a call a few days later telling me that it was all set.

We were going back to sunny California!

Chapter 18
1978 Back to California

Edie and I were both very excited to be going back to California. There was something special about the San Francisco Bay Area that clicked with both of us. Perhaps what attracted us so strongly was the fact that we were going to live there for so many years. I often think that my future life has an effect on my present life, like a giant resonator that supports and amplifies vibrations in a certain direction, toward an individual, or toward a particular line of thought. Of course I feel that I am free to follow the force, go with the flow, or to choose to go another way. But I must admit that I have almost always chosen to follow this inner guide, and when I chose not to follow it, life had a tendency to get into a tangle, if you know what I mean.

* * *

During the week after returning from DCI, I received a request from Dennis Delucia to do a brass clinic with the Long Island Sunrisers in preparation for the DCA championships to be held in Allentown, Pennsylvania on September 3rd. I had never worked with a senior corps before. As a matter of fact, I hadn't even seen a senior drum corps since I left the Skyliners in 1965. I decided to take the clinic because I knew it would help me to get my thinking straight and to find out if my bag of tricks was complete enough to face a rowdy bunch of screaming east coast volume pumpers.

During the five days of rehearsal that I spent with the Sunrisers I used every trick in my bag. I found myself inspired by the performers' zeal and enthusiasm to improve. The Sunrisers were a very pleasant surprise. Winning the DCA title was a pleasant surprise too. By the time I returned home I was totally hyped about the prospects of teaching the Blue Devils.

I was ready!

* * *

It was time to sell our house!

We put a little money into sprucing up the grounds so that it might sell more quickly. Our departure date was set for the weekend before Thanksgiving so there was much to be done and not much time to do it.

Now that Edie was a banker she knew all about the housing market, and she made a great estimate as to what the house might sell for. Everyone who was in the know told her she was too high on her asking price but she stuck to her guns and we made a quick killing. We realized more income from the sale of that house than I had made in my whole life teaching drum corps.

Edie was a salesman and I was playing with wooden toys…

I flew out to Concord in late October to scout the area and find a nice house in a quiet neighborhood. Something that was close to all the things we would be needing. I wanted to have everything ready to start our new life as soon as we pulled in, unpacked, and found a good stereo store. Yea! I hadn't had a real component stereo since we left the Acoustic Research equipment in Midwest, Wyoming in the spring of '73. Five years is a long time to go without the big, clear sound.

One more time we packed up the family car, which now happened to be a new red Datsun 510 wagon. Our blue F10 had been severely damaged by golf ball size hail, and the insurance company came through with a big settlement.

We managed to fill to overflowing a large U-Haul truck with everything we owned except for Timmy's rocking horse, which he still misses. There was just no more room left for it anywhere. Daphne the Great Dane was not going with us back to California. She had died peacefully in the back yard on a warm summer day.

Part Two

Blue Devils

Chapter 19
1979 Blue Devils

I have never been one to rush into things. I prefer to observe the lay of the land, see how things are going down before jumping in with both feet.

I'm the kind of guy who wants to know where I'm going before I put the car in gear. Once I know where I'm going, and what must be done, I formulate plans and strategies that will work best in given situations.

That is why, at my first Blue Devil rehearsal, when asked which section of the brass line I would like to work with I answered, "the contrabasses." I prefer to start at the bottom and work my way up.

I remember going outside that evening with the contrabasses and rehearsing under a lamppost in the Mt. Diablo High School parking lot. We all had a good time getting to know one another while focusing sounds, and learning to listen more closely, concentrating mainly on the sections of music that would be gone over in the full ensemble rehearsal.

The full ensemble rehearsal that evening, as I recall, was a master class in how not to make friends and influence people.

The experience was not what I had been hoping for in my fondest dreams!

I found the brass caption head's approach negative and demeaning. The soprano section was treated with such sarcasm that I honestly thought they might all quit at the end of rehearsal.

I know I would have!

But I had come to the Blue Devils to create my ultimate hornline.

I knew very well that Concord, California was the only place on earth where I would have the opportunity to make that dream come true. So I vowed to myself that I would wage a peaceful, silent, war on demeaning negativity and promote a positive, supportive environment in the Blue Devil brass program.

At the beginning of the next rehearsal I was asked to work with both the soprano line and the contrabass section.

Oh boy, here we go!

As I remember it, we played a few open tone warm-ups together before the contrabasses went out to work on their feature sections in the *Chicago III Suite*. The soprano section and I continued to warm up, but between exercises I told them that they could control and shape the ensemble rehearsal, that they had one chance and one chance only to turn the tide of rehearsal toward the hot and happy side.

They had to nail their part the very first time!

They had to nail it every time!

We proceeded to clear up any questions about the music we were rehearsing. The soprano section learned to sing the music, applying an articulation pattern to each section, repeating and repeating until it was both memorized and comfortable. They then played the part together, softly and slowly until each chord rang with assurance.

We spent some time tuning the instruments and then played a few loud chords to open up the sound and get the instruments vibrating. I told the soprano line that they had one chance to register a blow-away at the ensemble rehearsal, and that there was no time like the present to learn how to produce on demand.

I counted them off, knowing that I had set the situation up well and that the energy in the room was just beginning to crackle. They performed with a new sense of oneness, with positive energy that had not been obvious the week before, and when they performed that evening at the ensemble rehearsal they delivered the message loud and clear that the soprano line was there to play.

Bit by bit, my time with the full brass ensemble increased. I eventually had forty-five minutes with the full brass ensemble at the beginning of every brass rehearsal, for a warm up and bopping session. I wrote a whole new set of exercises designed to raise awareness in all of the technical areas of brass playing.

Bopping was something I had picked up in 1976 when I visited Fred Sanford at a Madison Scouts rehearsal in Colorado. Fred and I were heading toward the practice field to check out the marching rehearsal. What I heard was the sound of brass playing short, light notes. The music they were playing was understandable but there was no duration to the sounds. I asked Fred what they were doing and he said that they were playing attacks only, but past that he didn't know much about it. The idea stuck in my head and I began using it with both the 27th Lancers and the Sunrisers.

By the time I taught the bopping technique to the Blue Devils I had streamlined it so that slurred passages would be highly exposed and individualized. The technique of bopping involved playing a light attack on every note and immediately releasing it as though it were a staccato eighth note. The release was soft, not hard, open, not closed. Slurred passages were played with full duration sound until the last note of the slur, which was released as though it were an eighth note. Once the hornline became proficient at bopping it became possible to rehearse for long periods of time without over taxing lip muscles. It was their brains that were working hardest: to make sense of music in a new context. It took quite a bit of awareness to bop without blowing it, and when somebody blew it, everyone knew it.

* * *

I flew to Montreal twice that winter to work with Les Chatelaines, an all girl corps.

I had to learn French to communicate with the brass players!

But before I learned to say a few key phrases, a wonderfully loud gentleman with a pronounced lisp translated my every utterance to the performers. I found the experience strange! It was difficult to get on a roll when I had to stop and wait for the wonderfully loud gentleman to give his translation.

On one of my visits with the Chatelaines we were all mysteriously led into a darkened, seemingly empty, room. The brass players formed a circle around various small pieces of equipment located in the center of the room. Whatever this activity was going to be it was obvious that everyone, with the exception of yours truly, had done it before.

Everyone was speaking French so I had no idea what was being said or what was going to happen. Suddenly a large, bright, bulb began flashing in the center of the room. It held a steady pulse, commands were given and the brass players began playing in perfect sync with the flashing bulb.

Amazing! Using a precise visual stimulus for tempo control as opposed to an audio beat.

I have no idea how long one would care to stare into that bright, flashing light but it did seem to be an interesting and productive idea.

In all my years in drum corps I had never seen a metronome being used in any way what so ever, that is until I experienced the flashing white light in Montreal.

* * *

The Blue Devil staff in 1979 was in a state of flux. Jim Ott, who had been the brass caption head since 1972, left the corps at the end of the 1977 season, and Rick Odello, who had been percussion caption head since the corps' beginning, left the corps at the end of 1978. Frank Dorritie, who had taught brass with Wayne Downey in 1978, did not return for the '79 season.

Fewer than half of the 1978 soprano line had returned for the '79 season, and that number included only two lead sopranos. There existed a similar situation in the rest of the brass line, whereas the color guard and percussion sections were solid with veterans from past years.

The competitive show for 1979 was a great show for brass. *Chicago III Suite*, a hold over from 1978, worked well as the first half of the '79 show. The 1950's Stan Kenton tune *La Suerte de los Tontos* (Ship of Fools) filled the bill as a truly hot concert production. The exciting drum solo of *Pauper in Paradise* by Gino Vanelli led dramatically into the beautiful closer *My Heart Belongs To Me* by Barbra Streisand.

It was quite a cross section of American music!

You might wonder which hip Blue Devil staff member was aware of a Barbra Streisand recording and you would be right in doing so. The person who came up with *My Heart Belongs To Me* was none other than my lovely wife Edie, who has always been a devoted Barbra Streisand fan.

I came home one evening from a staff meeting and told Edie that the staff was having a problem picking a closing production for the show. The Blue Devils hadn't had a great closer since 1976 when they played *Chase The Clouds Away* by Chuck Mangione.

I still recall Edie sitting me down and telling me that she had a great song for the Blue Devils. She cued the track up and left me to listen.

Edie was right. The tune had just the right feel, with a lusty soprano solo, and a great soprano feature; and happily for the visual designers, it led perfectly into "the gates," a signature drill event at the end of Blue Devil shows.

So I brought the album with me to the next staff meeting, being very careful not to let anyone see the cover. If they did they might not have let me in. When the time came I cued the track and got out of the way. It was a resounding success, well maybe not resounding, but it went over well enough to gain it the closer spot in the show.

The overall tenor of Blue Devil staff meetings came very close to what one might describe as a state of anarchy. If you didn't know that Jerry Seawright was the corps' director you might have thought he was the jovial host at a party. Jerry brought the refreshments. But it was obvious that Jerry took everything in, and when necessary, did his best to referee when there were clashes between factions of the staff.

This same chaotic state of one-upmanship between staff members also held true at rehearsals, and it didn't matter if there were large groups of local population present. Everyone on the creative staff seemed equal in their ability to take over center stage and flex their muscles.

Two of the key staff members in 1979 had been soprano players in the Santa Clara Vanguard during the two years I taught there in the late '60s. One of them had been my high G whiz kid (he asked me what he should do since he hadn't yet memorized his music, so I told him to watch me and play a high G whenever I pointed at him... He actually did it!) and the other one had great difficulty finding the time to memorize his fingerings for *Procession of the Nobles*.

A third member of the staff had been the lead snare drummer for the Casper Troopers when I taught there in the late '60s. And one of the marching staff members had started his drum corps career with the Troopers and went on to become one of the finest baritone soloists I had ever heard.

There was no doubt about it, Jerry Seawright's instructional staff was intense, creative, stubborn, and many times unaware of the impact their words and actions had on other staff members, corps members, and onlookers alike. But Jerry Seawright maintained a loose rein for a reason. He did what few drum corps directors would be willing to do; he allowed the staff the freedom to do what they thought best.

* * *

One of my favorite diversions when working with the full brass ensemble was tagged "Space Music." The idea originally came from a scene I had observed from the window of a Trooper bus in the early '70s. A hornline was standing in a warm-up arc and the instructor was somehow changing the sound of the ensemble by sweeping his hand from one side of the line to the other. That was all I saw and heard before the bus pulled away and the vision was gone. I never knew what corps it was or the name of the instructor involved but I would like to thank him publicly for the idea.

Space Music became my way of attracting the attention of each and every performer to the movements of my hands. An ever-growing number of chords could be wiped on, or wiped off of the ensemble with a variety of hand signals. There were short snippets of melody from movies and TV shows like *Close Encounters* and *The Twilight Zone* that could be signaled at any moment, and all of this was done with hand signals.

Space Music also became the big hype for the before show warm-ups. It was a great way to lock in the tuning, and raise very high levels of fun-loving volume, so it was ideal as a preparation for full out performance.

* * *

The Blue Devil organization was amazing in so many ways. There was the A corps, the B corps, a variety of twirler and majorette groups, as well as senior and junior drum and bell corps, and each unit presented their show at the family night celebration.

In addition to the many performing groups in the organization there were the dedicated people who ran the bingo game without which the Blue Devil A corps could not exist. There was the board of directors, the food crew, the bus drivers, maintenance crew, field crew and the folks who ran the souvenir wagon.

And then there were the wonderful moms who took care of everything else.

For the most part, winter music rehearsals were held in local school gymnasiums or multipurpose rooms. But being that we were in California we could rehearse outside much of the year.

The Blue Devils had their own outdoor rehearsal facility, which was called Mars. It was called Mars because it was hot in the daytime and cold at night and always windy. The soil was basically dried up clay and consequently cracked and separated in strange patterns and there wasn't a tree or bush in sight.

By the time I came to the Blue Devils the field crew had made inroads to making it almost livable with a few trees, some grass, lights, and a GE box that teetered and tottered between four telephone poles. Going up the shaky metal frame to get to the box on a cold night with the wind blowing could be a very scary experience indeed.

Chapter 20
Blue Devil Blowaways

Zig Kanstul built twenty-six large bore, two-valve, silver King Sopranos (complete with a special slip slide that could be used to tune any note) for the Blue Devils in 1979. As soon as they arrived I loaded all twenty-six of them into my little red wagon and took them home to meet the strobe.

The better part of a week was spent tuning and testing the instruments until they played the same, felt the same, and sounded the same. When I was satisfied, I scribed each of them with what I call a main tuning mark on the main tuning slide.

Once the main tuning mark had been scribed, it was necessary to scribe a series of incremented marks on the main tuning slide. This way the instruments could be kept in tune when changes of temperature made it necessary to shorten or lengthen them. If temperatures went up the instruments had to be lengthened and if temperatures went down the instruments had to be shortened in order to maintain the pitch of A=440. I believe the reason for this phenomenon is that vibrations tend to move slower in cold air and faster in hot air. Speed of vibration is what determines pitch.

I decided to standardize soprano mouthpieces in order to strengthen the ring of overtones. Overtones are a series of audible vibrations, which accompany the sound of a single note, and when they are strengthened and supported through mutual resonance they tend to ring. I chose to go with the Claude Gordon line because their mouthpieces had a clear sound and a good solid center. I found it necessary to bore out the throats of the mouthpieces because they have a tendency to lose their proper dimensions due to heavy plating.

By the second camp of the year I'd sat down with each instrument in the hornline and match tuned it to each of the other instruments. All of the horns were tuned, marked, and tested.

I found that once the instrument tuning was complete it was necessary to work the performers into the centers of their instruments by doing unison pitch bending and pedal tones as well as octaves, fifths, and chords.

I kept a notebook with every instrument listed, showing both the performer's name and the actual measurement of the main tuning mark. From then on, each time we tuned, which usually meant a quick run down the line while matching tones, any deviations were minutely adjusted and the change was marked in the book. The beauty of this system was that once the bugs were all worked out the performers could always expect to be in fine tune.

This way of tuning brass instruments added a very special ingredient to the mix: consistency. It also meant that we didn't have to spend time tuning in order to be in tune. This added yet another important ingredient to the brass program: efficiency. All I had to do was tell the lead players what marks to set to and off we would go, in tune.

"Always remember… nothing, but nothing, takes the place of fine intonation!"
Philip Farkas

* * *

It felt good to be using the wealth of knowledge and experience I had gathered from so many wonderful and talented people throughout my life. I was giving it back, paying it forward!

* * *

In addition to three rehearsals a week, a three-day camp each month, staff meetings, and many hours assisting with arranging and copying, I gave private lessons to whoever wanted to take them. Mostly the students were soprano players. They took their lessons on trumpet, which was a good reason for me to get my trumpet chops in shape.

I had to learn to scream with the best of them!

The first difficulty I found with practicing every day was consistency of lip sensitivity from day to day. Some days my lips felt great. Other days they felt like a piece of dried-out cowhide. On days when my lips felt good I was able to accomplish much in the way of establishing fluid strength. But on bad lip days it never felt good. It would sometimes get a little better through the day but usually not.

I remember thinking to myself that things could not go on this way; I had to figure out a way of having the same set of lips show up from one day to the next. I decided to try warming up in stages.

After my morning ritual I would go out to the kitchen and put water on for tea. I would then pick up the trumpet and lightly noodle around on pedal tones and whatever came to mind for maybe five minutes. Maybe only three minutes. Then I would put the trumpet down, make my tea, and read through the music I would be playing later on. Or perhaps read a few pages of inspirational prose. Or meditate, as in clearing my mind of extraneous thoughts, which is always a good idea before entering into a new or different activity.

I would then go back to the trumpet and play a few open tone patterns with pedals, perhaps spend a few minutes on light improvisation and then put the horn back down.

During this time I paid little critical attention to how my lips were feeling.

I was just going through the process!

Five or ten more minutes of reading, or doing yoga, or watering the garden, and then it's back to the trumpet. So far, maybe twenty-five minutes into the warm-up, my lips are about where they should be and I am ready to start practicing.

This was the system that worked for me. It was a simple but effective process. By the time I finished my tea and watering I was warmed up and ready to go, with the same good set of lips showing up day after day.

* * *

Armed with the evidence of the flashing light in Montreal, I brought my trusty Taktell metronome to rehearsal one evening. The rehearsal was at Mars. I climbed the rickety old metal ladder and entered the box. It was one of those beautiful evenings that come along from time to time during early spring in Northern California. It was calm, the temperature was perfect, and the full corps was on the field under the lights.

I took my metronome out of my pocket and opened it up. Someone asked if I was going to play the piano. The big problem was that the metronome had to sit on something level and there was not a level piece of two by four anywhere. So I had to hold it level.

I listened to the next count-off by the drum major, checked my score for a tempo marking, set the Taktell and immediately noticed a discrepancy. The count off was slower than the tempo marking.

I pointed this out to the other staff members in the box, and by the end of that night's rehearsal the mighty Taktell was being held level by one person while someone else positioned the microphone up to it so that the whole corps could hear it go tick- tock before the drum major's count off.

Efficiency! Don't you just love it? Eventually we all had Dr. Beats or small, pocket size electronic metronomes that had just recently been made available on the market in the late seventies.

* * *

It was summer, and time for Timmy to learn to ride a bicycle. I found a used bike at a garage sale, brought it home, stripped it down, cleaned and lubricated it, replaced the tires, painted it Tim's favorite color, orange, and inscribed his name on the front where the insignia usually goes. Tim loved his bike. I also built him a large ferry boat like the ones I had ridden to Staten Island when I was a kid, complete with ramps, cars, and ferry boat captain.

Life was good. I was busy but not too busy. I had time to investigate and create.

I had time to cook!

I love to cook. For me cooking is a creative endeavor, like painting a picture or writing a song. I had cookbooks but never followed the recipes. I read the recipes to see what ingredients were used but that was all.

There was one exception, however. When we were living in Laramie, Wyoming, Edie bought for me a great Italian cookbook. In it there was a recipe for Lasagna Verde, which Edie and I made together for a gathering of friends and family.

Edie preferred that we follow the recipe, exactly!

I have to admit that it was the best-tasting lasagna I had ever eaten, but I never made it the same way again.

I guess I have a problem with restrictions. I don't mind self-restriction within reason. Free and easy, that's my style, howdy do me, watch me smile!

I don't like to be told what to do, I don't like to follow other cars in a caravan, and I have no desire to do the same thing day after day. I like variety. I would rather create something new than do the same old thing the same old way.

I think that what I am is a creative introvert!

I know I am an introvert
I create my world from within
I enjoy having choices to make, directions to take
Mostly I learn from doing, which always raises questions
Questions that compel me to explore the growing world of knowledge in books
I learn from quiet introspection
I learn from success
I learn from mistakes
I learn from watching children
How they sit and how they stand
I learn from observing the world around me
Life is a learning experience, and it has taught me to
Enjoy being alive and to expect the unexpected

* * *

I loved working with the young people who came to perform with the Blue Devils. They were full of energy and eager to learn; that is, once you gained their respect and attention. I was interested in how they responded differently to various members of the staff, and found it easy to change their mood from negative to positive when necessary. I have always believed in the power of positive thinking. It only makes sense to move in positive directions, it's the best way to get to where you want to go.

So when it came time to go out onto the practice field to make performance tapes of the hornline as they played and marched through the routine, I balked at the idea of doing a "tic" tape. A tic tape is a recording the instructor makes of the mistakes he hears while walking through the moving drill formations, many times making note, on the tape, of the performers who he thinks made the errors.

I didn't wish to pick the hornline's performance apart; I wanted to encourage the idea of going for it. I wanted them to blow me away with their power, energy, and musicianship. I wanted them to encourage each other with their playing, and to feel good about themselves and their accomplishments.

So I came up with the idea of doing "blowaway" tapes. On a blowaway tape the instructor says things like "Whoa dude! That was cool", or "Oh my God, that was fantastic," things like that, and if you mentioned the people involved in the blowaway on the tape, they really got a kick out of it. The kids would pass the tapes around at night for entertainment.

* * *

Being on the road with a top drum and bugle corps had a certain sense of full time exhilaration for me. It was a feeling of being totally alive, like the corps itself was a living, breathing entity with only one desire: to be the best, to take on all comers, to drive the crowd to their feet. It was like that with the Troopers, it was like that with the Vanguard, it was like that with the Muchachos, and it was like that with the Blue Devils.

But how the Blue Devils traveled across the country was like nothing I had ever seen before. We had a staff bus with bunks to sleep in, a fully equipped food wagon that fed the corps (and staff) night and day, a giant equipment truck to carry all those instruments, uniforms, and color guard equipment, and out in front of the corps leading us all merrily down the road we had Jerry Seawright in his flagship Tioga.

Jerry Seawright was a first-class kind of guy from the way he dressed to the way he treated people. He radiated a sense of supreme self-confidence that simply made one feel at ease and safe. Everything would be okay because Jerry was there. Whatever the staff or circumstances may have required, Jerry Seawright would find a way to supply what was needed, and he would always accomplish the task in a gentlemanly manner.

In my humble opinion, Jerry Seawright was a prince among men, and one hell of a drum corps director.

Chapter 21
1979 Two Blue Devil Shows

I specifically remember two shows from the 1979 season. One was in Whitewater, Wisconsin, the home of the first DCI World Championship competition in 1972. I had been somehow able to finagle my way up to the very top of the general effect box. It was a great place from which to experience a drum corps show, truly a bird's eye view. I was about fifteen feet above the crowd, just high enough to catch the wash of sound as it came up over the top of the box.

Brass players are taught to aim the bell of their instrument at the GE Box, as it is called, and blanket it with sound. Consequently, I was the uppermost beneficiary.

Being that far above the roar of the crowd diminished their noise level sufficiently so as not to be distracting. I was way up above the field. It was like looking down at the street from the rooftop of my apartment building in the Bronx.

What I recall so vividly about the Blue Devils' performance that evening was that at times everything clicked together, the entire effect was simultaneous: one hundred and thirty performers all working in perfect sync with one another. There were no distractions, flubs, or rubs to keep the observers from becoming completely mesmerized by the musical kaleidoscope being created on the field before them.

The show would lock together for maybe as long as fifteen or twenty seconds before a glitch would suddenly break the spell. After a momentary shake the corps would lock together again, restoring my attention to the entirety of the spectacle.

By the end of the performance I was both elated and mystified by what I had experienced. I was elated because the idea of holding a crowd of thousands in a rapt hypnotic state had been a goal of mine since that night in 1954 when I was so affected by the performance of Frankie Farr and the Appleknockers. I was mystified by what I'd observed because I had no idea what it was going to take for the corps to exist in a state of total absorption, living and breathing as one, from the first note of the show to the last.

This concept of locking together was one that occupied my mind for quite some time after my Whitewater experience. I likened the concept of 'locking together' to the mind-altering effects of chant and fire dance rituals: people coming together to achieve more than the sum of their own individual efforts, to experience the power of unity, to act and feel as one, one mind, one desire, one goal.

* * *

The second show, which is indelibly hard-wired into my memory from 1979, is the Blue Devils' DCI finals performance in Birmingham, Alabama. I watched the corps file into the stadium that night from only a few feet away and took notice of the expressions on the individual faces as they passed by. The intensity was obvious in every one of them. All of the performers had the same steady gaze of determination finely etched into the landscape of their features. Even Scott Johnson, the lead snare drummer, whose eyes would usually be checking everything out in sight, had taken on a steadier, more resolute demeanor. Needless to say, I was impressed.

When the last member of the corps had gone by, I took off on a beeline for the stands. This was one performance I was not going to miss. I headed for the fifty-yard line, about half way up the lower deck. I had already scoped out a possible viewing place during the preliminary competition, which, by the way, the corps had won, edging out the Phantom Regiment by a mere one tenth of a point.

The stadium was packed. Every seat was taken, but I had expected that. I found the perfect spot to squat down where no one seemed to mind. The familiar voice of Brandt Crocker had just begun announcing the corps as I settled down. The year flashed through my mind, and what a year it was. Step by step the performers had matured to the point that

I had to re-imagine my ultimate hornline; they had already reached the goal I had set for them.

The idea of locking together served me well. I figured out that a great part of the locking together process involved getting everyone in perfect sync by becoming wholly present in the here and now.

On tour, the hornline and I did yoga every day, which included short meditations. The meditations were based on self-hypnosis concepts useful for relaxing the body and calming the mind. It was like taking the performers on a short mental holiday, clearing and refreshing their thought processes.

And so here we were at the final competition of the year and the kids from Concord were about to show the drum corps world what they had learned.

The drum major gave the count-off (absolutely perfect tempo) and the percussion came in with a bang that started everything moving at close to two hundred beats per minute. I can only tell you that the first note from the brass was absolutely glorious to my ears. It was clear, powerful, musical, totally energized, and compelling. Tears came to my eyes as a feeling of tremendous power surged through my body. It was all I could do to keep from jumping up and roaring at the top of my lungs. The sound was everything that I had ever dared to imagine and more.

The corps was magnificent, the brass was captivating, and happily the judges agreed with my assessment. That night the Blue Devils were awarded the highest final score in DCI history. We won the brass caption with the second highest score in DCI history (second only to the '75 Madison Scouts by one and one half tenths).

I was in drum corps heaven. Completely satisfied... for the moment.

But lurking somewhere in the back of my mind was that old nagging thought that returned again and again, "What now?" "What's next?"

Chapter 22
1980 Blue Devil C and Bridgemen

In September of 1979 I went to Jerry Seawright and proposed that we start a C drum and bugle corps, by adding a hornline to the existing Blue Devil drum and bell corps that I had seen perform at family night. The drum and bell corps age range was from 6 to 12. All we had to do was purchase twelve G bugles, without valves, which I had already scoped out with Zig Kanstul. I also proposed that I oversee the technical side of the Blue Devil brass program by instructing all three corps, A B and C.

Poor Jerry. I could see on his face the worry about financial outlay. He actually struggled with the dilemma right before my eyes. I knew he wanted to do it, first of all because it would be a good thing for the organization, and secondly because he knew I really wanted to do it. My sons John and Tim were the perfect ages to begin their drum corps careers. Jerry said to order the horns and that he would find a way to do it if he had to pay for them himself.

Thank God for Jerry Seawright!

The G bugles were delivered in early December. John and Tim accompanied me to attend the first official brass rehearsal of the Blue Devil C Corps, and to open the big square box that was waiting for us. The horns were wrapped in plain brown paper, this was a shoestring operation, no cases, no frills, but they were all bright and shiny and came complete with Claude Gordon mouthpieces.

Thank you, Zig Kanstul.

By January 1980 we had 12 buglers coming to rehearsal each week.

Everyone started with a mouthpiece. They learned how to hold it properly, how to breathe and blow air through the mouthpiece properly, how to set the mouthpiece properly on their lips, and how to buzz the sound of a siren sounding from far away, to close up, and far away again. They learned to play *Popeye the Sailor Man* complete with the Toot Toot on the end. When they could play Popeye on their mouthpiece, while standing up straight and holding the mouthpiece properly, they would be given a shiny new bugle.

I made individual awards for each C corps rehearsal. They were created with colored paper, pens and stickers. The awards were for best high note, best low note, best tone, best posture, longest note, etc. etc. Then there were the awards for the best of the night, super horn, star, and hero, etc. John and Tim would pick their favorite award before leaving for practice, and then try to win it during rehearsal that evening.

In time, the boys made the awards themselves, each vying for the favorite pick of the evening. (When it came time during rehearsal to give out the awards there was usually one award that was favored by everyone, and that was the one the boys were trying to create: everyone's favorite award!)

Speaking of favorite awards, the first place trophy and the high brass award at DCI last summer had a stronger effect on my psyche than I would ever have imagined. My self-confidence level was bolstered; I took up more space in the world. I felt ever so slightly larger than life. I think it was a good thing, like the gentle jab of a spur on my rump.

I wanted more!

I wanted to do more, I wanted to learn more, I wanted to go further, I wanted to create a monster of a hornline.

So I wrote new exercises, more challenging exercises, more fun exercises, exercises that demanded the performers' full attention. I had been spurred on by my realization during the past season that the idea of locking together was to a large extent linked with being acutely aware of yourself and your immediate environment as the future comes crashing into the present. I wanted to promote living in the present moment so fully that all else would fade: no distractions, complete experience.

So we did things like "milling around." Milling around was first performed on the infield of a baseball diamond just across the dirt road from Mars. I had the hornline spread out into an area roughly between the pitcher's mound and the backstop. They then spaced themselves equally and chose which direction to face. I had them do a slow turn in place with their instruments up in playing position to see how they were situated in respect to everyone else. There were over sixty brass players involved in this exercise; there wasn't a whole lot of room between them.

Once they had a good idea of their situation I explained what was going to happen. They were to play a certain section of music at a soft volume level and stay in motion as they did it. No one was to bump into anyone else. Contrabasses had the right of way. No fast moves, total awareness of themselves in an ever-changing environment. They were to mill around.

It was one of the funniest things I ever saw!

Musical cattle!

They loved it. Once they got the hang of it they played the piece at full volume, while milling around, and blew themselves away. The sound from outside of the form was amazing: a constantly changing mix of voices within a full-bodied ensemble texture. I did not dare go inside of that living jukebox to see what it was like for them. I contented myself with remaining on the outer limits.

Du di du do du di du do, du-dl-e-ding

* * *

The repertoire for 1980 was *Ya Gotta Try* (Buddy Rich), *Pegasus* (Hank Levi), *Free* (Chicago), *La Suerte de los Tontos* (Stan Kenton), *Pauper in Paradise* (Geno Vanelli) and *Dindi* (pronounced Gingi) as performed by the Singers Unlimited. It was another powerful show, and soloist paradise.

As far as I was concerned nothing beat a great solo performed by a great soloist, and we had more than our share of great solos and great soloists in 1980. The two individuals who performed the solos in the closing production of *Dindi* were definitely the most professional sounding "buglers" I have ever heard.

They were extremely convincing! And musical! And they were each very intense individuals in their own way. You can hear subtle differences in the personality of their playing but not in the quality of their sound.

The Blue Devil soprano lines were an inspiration to me. They worked harder and believed more strongly in themselves than any group of people I had ever worked with. They continually surprised and amazed me with their ability to grow and mature.

The success of the soprano line's performances of 1979 attracted a number of fine high brass players to our tryouts. After all, who wouldn't want to play with a group like that? Even I loved playing in the line when I got the chance. Playing with the soprano section on a regular basis gave me the sense of power I needed to break open my upper register.

The 1979 upper lead sopranos worked many hours in front of a strobe learning to match each other's sound and pitch in the upper register. They didn't love doing it but the results were worth working for.

* * *

In January of 1980 I received a call from Bobby Hoffman, the director of the Bridgemen from Bayonne, New Jersey. He asked if I would come out east to do a clinic with the Bridgemen hornline and maybe have some fun while I was at it. Bobby was always up for some fun.

I mention the clinic because I realized something during the clinic that I had never before occasioned to notice. I had become so used to the intonation characteristics of the Blue Devil line that it was extremely difficult for me to go about working with the Bridgemen without at least trying to tune their instruments, if for no other reason than to assess the instruments' condition. It didn't make any sense to ask for musical qualities when much of ensemble musicianship is dependent upon tone matching and proper intonation. Of course it was impossible to achieve the tuning I had become used to but I did my best. The thing I realized during these rehearsals was that it was so much more difficult to bring about the improvement I was hoping for. The resonance of a finely tuned ensemble encourages musicality in a way that nothing else does.

Consider if you will the difference between playing on a beautifully tuned piano and an out of tune piano. It would be comically uncouth to attempt a sensitive rendition of *Moonlight Sonata* on an out of tune piano, no matter the expertise of the performer. One should feel the same way about a brass ensemble.

* * *

The Blue Devils won every show that year with the exception of one, and that was DCI East in Allentown, PA. The east coast was coming on strong. The 27th Lancers had put together a very exciting show featuring drill designs by George Zingali. The Bridgemen had a dynamite show designed by Bobby Hoffman. Dennis Delucia's percussion was powerful and spotless. Spirit of Atlanta, with the music of Jim Ott, was right on everyone's heels.

After our loss in Allentown we were on our way to Charlotte and somehow became separated from our equipment truck, which left us stranded with no instruments. No instruments meant no rehearsal, and no rehearsal meant idle hands and minds.

The hornline let me know that they wanted to talk to me. They were totally bummed. One of the staff members had said that the powers that be were not going to let the Blue Devils win this year.

The "kids" were all acting very down and grim.

I told them that thinking negatively was not going to do them any good. Thinking positively would brighten their self-image and make them strong. I reminded them of the fact that they were the finest hornline in the world, and had been for two years running. I said that if they were truly going to roll over and die just because someone said that a nebulous "they" were not going to let the Blue Devils win this year, then I would consider myself free to return home and spend some well deserved time with my family.

We did some yoga, took a short but refreshing mental vacation, and ended up with a fairly serious running block. I told them during the running block, "between now and tomorrow night in Charlotte you must each find at least one way to improve your own personal show, and you can be sure that I will do the same."

The Blue Devils won the Charlotte show with by far the best performance of the year and received their first 90 of the season. It was a 90.050. Our score at DCI semi-finals that week in Birmingham Alabama was 90.400, and our final score at DCI was 90.600. In the final competition, the Blue Devils tied for sixth place in percussion, took second place in marching, second place in general effect, and ran away with first place in brass by a large enough margin to win the show by three and a half tenths of a point.

Whew!

It was a great win, mainly because our competition was so good. Dennis Delucia's magnificent Bridgemen drumline took high percussion, along with Spirit of Atlanta. The 27th Lancers took high general effect, and Phantom Regiment was awarded high marching. And for the first time in history, the east coast took three of the top four spots at the DCI final competition.

* * *

On July 8th 1980 Jim Ott was killed in an auto related accident while touring with the Spirit of Atlanta. He will always be remembered with love and gratitude.

Chapter 23
Blue Devils Combined Hornlines

In the fall of 1980 we held a special meeting at our house. The C corps staff was getting together to re-invent the newly created drum corps. A complete change of uniform was the topic.

The traditional uniform of the drum and bell corps had been white shoes, light blue pants and shako, white satin blouse with red ascot and cummerbund.

Edie and I had an idea to add the Spanish influence, suggested in the name Mount Diablo or Devils Mountain, which is a huge singular eruption of earth, peaking out at an altitude of 3,849 feet, located just to the southeast of Concord.

Our idea was to go gaucho! A royal blue sleeveless, embroidered vest and pants, trimmed in red and white, with red gaucho inserts in the cuffs. White satin blouse with red cummerbund and a very comfortable flat brimmed gaucho hat in blue with a red band. By the end of the meeting the staff was in agreement about the idea so it was put into action.

The new Blue Devil C corps was born!

* * *

Edie now held the position of lead secretary for the district branch manager of Bank of America in downtown Concord. She was moving up in the world of finance, so much so that I was able to buy a 1966 Sunbeam Alpine, in great shape. I had sold my old Alpine to Edie's brother Marv when we moved back to New Jersey, but here I was scootin' around with the top down, with a fantastic stereo system pumping out great sounds from the 60s and 70s. We were living the good life, that was for sure.

John and Tim were busy going to school, playing little league baseball and marching with the Blue Devil C corps. Edie was working nine to five at the Bank of America and taking classes at the local JC. I was doing my morning ritual of tea, trumpet warm-up and practice. There were meetings and arranging sessions in the late mornings, and individual lessons scattered sporadically throughout the day. I had only recently taken over cooking responsibilities from Edie and I was into making soups, pasta, and chili.

One day while I was getting ready to make a fresh batch of spaghetti sauce, my seven-year-old son Tim asked if I would read him a story. I had been waiting for just such an opportunity and decided to capitalize on Tim's affinity for folktales, fables, and mythology. My plan was to begin reading one of my favorite folktales to Tim, but just when the plot reached its most captivating moment I would have to excuse myself to take care of my spaghetti sauce, leaving Tim with the book, a ton of curiosity, and the gnawing need to know what happens.

The thought behind the plan was to create a situation whereby the act of "reading" was simply the necessary means to satisfy Tim's desire to know or understand something.

We sat down and began reading. It was easy to sense Tim's imagination soaring as the action began to mount; and just as the hero was about to face his most dangerous challenge, I calmly excused myself to go fix dinner.

"What", said Tim, "you can't leave now. What am I gonna do?"

To this I simply shrugged my shoulders and suggested that he come and tell me what happens. I was careful to leave only a few pages so Tim wouldn't feel the task was too large.

By the time the sauce started to boil Tim came bursting into the kitchen bubbling over about how the story ended, exclaiming that this was his favorite story of all time.

Learning happens naturally when spurred on by desire. We all perform better when we are doing what we wish to do, as opposed to what we are told to do. Learning should be a natural consequence of a person's desire to do or to know.

* * *

We had a huge backyard with grapefruit, orange and almond trees, and lots of grass, which Edie had to goad me into mowing. You must remember that I was brought up in a New York apartment building, there was no grass, there was no mower, there was only concrete, and I had been slow to notice that the grass needed tending.

So Edie and I went to our local Sears store and bought our very first electric lawn mower, with a very long extension cord. As I said it was a really big backyard, but the boys loved having a big backyard to play baseball in.

From time to time I would hold soprano sectionals in the backyard. John and Tim thought that was great because they could look forward to a pitching or hitting lesson from Pete Burnejko. Pete was a baseball player turned soloist for the 1980 season, he was really great with the kids, and he was a fantastic soloist.

Speaking of soloists, I was blessed with many fine players who succeeded in blowing my socks off with some of the hottest solos in drum corps. One such individual was Larrie Dastrup, featured soloist with the Blue Devils in '79, '80, and '81. Larrie would come to C corps rehearsal and work with the players individually. Of course, all of the kids in the C corps hornline, my boys included, knew who Larrie was, and for him to come and give them a lesson was a real treat.

1981 was the first year of the combined hornlines at Blue Devil family night. During the afternoon of family night, the A, B, and C corps hornlines gathered together in the parking lot of Diablo Valley Junior College. One of the tunes I had written for the C corps was called *Stop Gap*. It was a simple tune with a light jazz flavor and used only the tones of the open G bugle, which are C, E, G, and a flat Bb in the upper register. I had also arranged an accompaniment for the A and B corps to play. So we worked all of that out and spent some time learning Space Music, which the A corps was very familiar with but the B and C corps had never experienced.

For the finale of the rehearsal I had the hornlines play part of their show for each other. When it came time for the A corps to play, I brought the ensemble into a circle and had the B and C corps sit down on the ground in the middle. The circle was about fifteen yards in diameter.

I don't know if you have ever experienced the sound of sixty-two brass up close and personal like that, but I can tell you that it is a thrill not soon to be forgotten, as I am sure the members of B and C corps would tell you. Their faces lit up like Christmas morning. Family night rehearsals and performances soon became one of my favorite experiences of the season.

I spoke to you a moment ago about having the hornline form into a circle. This was one of my favorite ways to work with the ensemble. My number one reason for working in a circle was intimacy. I could look into the performers' eyes and they could look into mine. I could speak to them in a congenial way. I could speak musically about musical issues. I could tell a joke, or make a comment about their last performance. In a circle everyone is equally communicative.

I changed the voicing of the circle in any number of ways to enhance musical understanding between individuals and sections. If I wanted everyone to key into the bass, then the contrabasses would be equally spread around the circle. If I wanted to create a power circle, I would start with the mellophones and lead sopranos integrated as one section of the circle. The lower sopranos, French horns and lead baritones integrated as a second section of the circle, and lower baritones, euphoniums, and contra basses integrated as the third section of the circle. That left me with three very strong voicings to mingle together, thereby creating a clearer picture in the performers' minds of how their part fit into the big picture, and how they could better support one another's musical efforts.

The idea of integrating a brass arc in a variety of ways was first pointed out to me by one of the most musical individuals I had ever known, John Simpson. This occurred back in the early seventies when John was working with the Hutchinson Skyriders. He had his hornline demonstrate several different voicings of the arc so I could hear the various qualities made more apparent by the physical arrangement of the brass players.

Working off of the idea that John had given me, I designed many variations of both the arc and the circle, all of which provided the performers with new experiences from which to learn and grow.

Perspective is determined by point of view

More points of view provide a more complete perspective

A more complete perspective broadens understanding

I was never a big talker when it came to teaching instrumental music. My methods were all about creating the proper conditions, conditions where learning and maturity could readily take place. The greater the variety of musical situations provided for the performers, the more they understood musical performance from an empirical point of view; acquiring knowledge and understanding through the natural experience of performing and accomplishing.

"While words do wonderfully suggest musical ideas, they quite as frequently clip the wings of inspiration, which, in instrumental music may soar upward almost without limit."

S. A. Emery.

Chapter 24
1981 Blue Devils

The Blue Devils' show in 1981 was something old, something new, definitely brassy and no doubt blue. The opening and closing of the show were almost the same as the previous year. The show's new sections were the concert production of *One More Time Chuck Corea* by Gene Puerling, and an out of concert production of *Johnny One Note* by Rodgers and Hart. The percussion solo was based on a piece by Shakti.

The staff seemed different going into the 1981 season. Perhaps the change was due to the fact that the Blue Devils had won four of the last five DCI World titles. I had only been with the Blue Devils for the last two titles, but believe me, winning back-to-back DCI championships was quite a head-trip.

I was never one for resting on my laurels, though. I guess if I had learned anything by that point in my life it was that winning was only based on what others thought of your work, whereas to me the only thing that really mattered was what I thought of my work, and there is no doubt that I was pleased with what I had accomplished. But I knew very well that you are only as good as your latest triumph, so there was much to be done if I was going to create the best brass ensemble ever to grace the field of competition.

Before I could do that I had to imagine how the Blue Devil brass performance could be improved over what I had heard from the '79 and '80 ensembles. It was time to go back to the drawing board.

I decided to augment the warm-up program. I arranged tunes for the hornline to sight read during our now expanded time at the beginning of rehearsals. The sight-reading was once again my attempt to provide the performers with new experiences as a musical ensemble. I added broader tempo variations and greater dynamic depth to the exercise routines. The ensemble that plays together stays together, but as far as drum corps is concerned, louder and faster is better.

* * *

I was becoming a more dynamic player myself, which I can only attribute to using correct procedures in my practice at home. But I had always had a problem with sight-reading. Being relaxed and aware while performing was something I knew to strive for, but I had never connected it with sight-reading. The ability to sight-read while remaining in a relaxed state proved to be a key acquisition for improving my own self-awareness skills.

I purchased a stack of new music, which was ranked from easy moderate to moderately difficult. I sat down with my trumpet, music stand, and trusty metronome. I would then take the topmost book from the pile and place it on the music stand, turn it to the first piece in the book, look it over for all the usual suspects, set the metronome speed, and adjust my posture to be loose and lifted.

With the feel of the music in my mind and a full breath of air in my body I would calmly begin to play. As soon as I noticed any build up of static tension or muscular holding I would stop, put the instrument down, turn the metronome off, breathe in deep and relax. I would just let my bones and muscles hang loose.

Then I would turn to the next piece of music, look it over, set the metronome, adjust my posture, breathe, and begin playing until I noticed any buildup of static muscular tension. I would then put the instrument down, turn the metronome off, breathe in deep and release tension throughout my body, turn the page and begin the process again. This went on for weeks until I could sight-read without becoming tense.

It was amazing what I could accomplish once I set my mind to doing it.

A moment ago I used the term "loose and lifted" in referring to my posture while playing. I found it an important concept and wrote a short poem to emphasize the importance of this awareness.

Loose and lifted that's how you want to be
So you won't show the bad effects of our old friend gravity
I say old friend because gravity is with us all the time
He keeps us down upon the earth
Which is usually just fine
When you brush or comb your hair he keeps it down upon your head
When you fall asleep at night he holds you in your bed
When it's time to go for a swim he keeps the water in the pool
And when you sit down on a stool he keeps you on it as a rule
So as you see he holds things down
He pulls them with his power
He works all day and all night too! Every minute, every hour…
So if you wish to keep your body tall the way it ought to be
You must LIFT your body's weight to keep from getting short, you see?
If you persist at this idea and follow it to conclusion
Your body will be happy to be free of postural confusion

* * *

I was spending a lot of time practicing in front of a mirror in those days. I found that if I set my trumpet angle correctly, which meant setting the mouthpiece so that it was flat against my top teeth when my lip was out of the way, I could just see over the bell, the bell being slightly to the left of center. By memorizing the image in the mirror I could standardize the trumpet's position in relation to my embouchure. That little trick offered me a real sense of consistency in my playing, which paid off big time when it came to endurance and accuracy.

Other practices that I felt were extremely beneficial were playing with pedal tones, and putting my head down below my waist, which I will explain in a moment.

The pedal tone is the fundamental or lowest note of a brass instrument. The pedal tone produces only one complete sound wave, and that one sound wave fills the instrument from one end to the other.

A brass player can lip the pedal tone down because the shape of the instrument allows for the waveform to become longer by bulging out the front of the bell.

The reason that it is difficult to push the pedal tone sharp is that the waveform will not be pulled back into the bell easily and has a great tendency to pop up to the first overtone, which is an octave above the pedal tone. The first overtone then produces two waves instead of one, each wave being half the length of the original wave.

I hope that was clear...

I amused myself with pedal tones by playing them in various ways. For instance, I would play pedal tones with only my top lip in the mouthpiece, or with only my bottom lip in the mouthpiece. It takes a while to gain control over the vibration but I eventually developed a smooth, consistent, vibration.

I would also play pedal tones, using both lips, while slowly moving the mouthpiece from one side of my mouth to the other. The aim was to always produce a nice bass quality.

I would play with a pedal tone for minutes at a time imitating the sound of a B29 approaching and leaving a strike zone.

I would do slow flips rising from the deepest part of the pedal tone and moving on up into the overtones, very slowly with a clear easy tone.

After doing pedals, or any exercises for that matter, I would put my head down below my waist and let my arms hang while holding the trumpet with both hands. I would concentrate on allowing my facial muscles to be pulled down by gravity, and I would let my shoulders hang loose from my back, neck, and ribcage.

The way to build strong, healthy muscle tissue is to work the muscle, then relax it. The idea of relaxing the muscle is to bring fresh blood to the tissues in order to refresh them. Putting the head down accomplishes that, and more, due to the fact that extra blood and oxygen are being pumped to the brain and facial tissues. About ten seconds with the head down is all it takes to refresh the muscle tissues.

Another trick was done with spaghetti.

I used many of these techniques with the Blue Devil hornline. This was a fun one and it served two purposes. First of all, I used the spaghetti to carry out the exercise that I had in mind, but secondly, a few of the brass players took the unused spaghetti home to cook for dinner. I always made sure to buy the family size package.

The spaghetti exercise was based on the idea that the aperture or hole in the lips through which air is blown should be formed open, and that the buzz actually occurs around the perimeter of the aperture. This is in contrast to the idea that the hole is blown open by the air stream and vibrates open and closed. The former method creates an open sound whereas the latter creates a stuffy sound, which means it doesn't carry. And I wanted all the sound to carry.

You begin this exercise by cleaning out your mouthpiece. You take a piece of spaghetti about eight inches long. You put your mouthpiece to your lips, put the spaghetti through the opening at the end of the shank, push it on through the throat of the mouthpiece, on into the cup, and at this point you encounter your lips. Play and hold a note while touching the lips with the spaghetti to sensitize around the aperture. Now you can push the spaghetti through the aperture and find the tip of your tongue. See if you can locate the tongue while articulating on the teeth. You should be able to buzz a steady tone while moving the spaghetti in and out through the buzzing aperture.

Opening apertures with the spaghetti trick is a way to add weight to the ensemble sound. Rounding the aperture at the center of the embouchure opens the sound at the release of the note. This allows the ensemble's sound to ring. When the sound rings it carries and projects.

Another way to add weight to the ensemble sound is to have a great contrabass section. The Blue Devil contra line had improved steadily from that first night in the parking lot at Mt. Diablo High. In 1980 they achieved a wonderful sound and style on the introduction to *Pegasus*. They had learned to breathe in strange places, meaning that each of the performers played a slightly different part.

I wanted the contrabass sound to be absolutely smooth and consistent. The players would systematically subtract notes from their individual parts and breathe during the missing notes. It took a while to get the technique down but once mastered the contrabass section was able to maintain a smooth, beautiful tone quality at any volume. We also had fewer problems with tempo, because the performers no longer had to gasp for air at the end of phrases.

An exercise that I found particularly good for developing the contrabass sound was to have them do circuits around a track. I learned the basic concept from Charlie Groh back in the very early '70s when he was working with the Anaheim Kingsmen.

The practice was performed on a quarter mile track. The contrabass section would form a comfortable mass so that they were close enough to hear each other but not too close. The performers knew what sections of music needed to be worked. They would start with perhaps a four bar figure, set the tempo, and proceeded merrily down the track playing the lick over and over with short rests in between repetitions. Meanwhile I would sit under a shady tree and keep tabs on the tempo.

For some reason the contrabass section really enjoyed this activity. They felt empowered by the fact that they could control the sound of their own section. They were highly motivated individuals and simply needed a way to settle themselves in.

* * *

One highlight of the '81 season included a two thousand mile road trip for John, Tim, and myself to Salem, Oregon, Tacoma, and Seattle, Washington. The three of us were riding in our little red wagon and were on tour with the Blue Devils. Our first day out on the road we found a huge billboard announcing Giant Dune Buggy Rides. Being that we were all red blooded American males we followed the sign, and a better thing we could not have done.

It was a total blast!

These dune buggies were large enough to hold twenty or more people, and they had giant balloon tires well over six feet high. It was the most fun ride any of us had ever experienced, even to this day.

The northwest tour went well for the Blue Devils. One thing became very apparent though, as time went by; we had a rehearsal guzzler in the show. The *Johnny One Note* production was overwritten in the areas of brass arrangement and drill design. It required the brass performers to keep pumping out the sound with extremes of range, volume, and rhythmic intensity, while moving through a three-ring circus drill that never stopped. The production was a nightmare. It sucked up valuable rehearsal time and left everyone feeling tired and frustrated.

On our way home from Seattle, I decided to pull over and park in the Prairie Creek Redwood State Park just north of Eureka, California. It was almost midnight and I was not going to attempt to make it home that night. So we pulled into a parking area and as I swung the car into a lonely parking spot we caught sight of a sign that said Beware of Bears, which John had to read aloud so Tim would hear it. We put the seats down in our little red wagon, got the pillows in order, stretched out and went to sleep.

Sometime in the middle of the night I felt a little tug on my hand, and when I opened my eyes, there was Tim sitting bolt upright staring out of the window. He looked at me with wide-open eyes and said, "so far so good, Dad!"

* * *

For the third year in a row we won the high brass award at DCI. The Blue Devils took first in GE, first in brass, second in marching, and ninth in percussion. The corps placed second to the Vanguard overall by three tenths of a point.

Chapter 25
Trager Work

More than once in my cooking career I concocted a meal in which the individual entrees were tasty in and of themselves, but when all was said and done, the meal just didn't click, it didn't flow, it didn't take you from here to there.

That was how I felt about the 1981 Blue Devil show. There was no sense of flow or continuity. I think the problem may have arisen from the design people believing their own press clippings. They were all quite young at the time and seemed to feel they could do anything.

I fully realized that if our percussion section had taken fourth or fifth place instead of ninth place we would have won the '81 DCI title, but I was convinced that there was more to it than that.

The 1981 show just didn't click well enough to carry the vote.

Again my "Aha" light went on!

The whole must be greater than the sum of the parts. If it is less, you are in trouble.

* * *

In the fall of '81 I took a course in what Californians refer to as bodywork. The bodies we worked on were human bodies, not automobile bodies, but the idea was the same: remove the dents and dings of everyday life; restore a natural glow of health.

Bodywork is not massage… not even close! Most forms of bodywork don't use oils. The bodywork I chose to study was called "Trager work," based on the work of Milton Trager.

Trager work is a movement-based form of bodywork, which has two components. The first is a passive session, called tablework, in which the practitioner takes each part of the client's body through its normal range of motion, but does it so gently and rhythmically that the client eventually relaxes deeply enough to let go of habituated patterns of stiffness and become more flexible. This sounds like it would be a lot of work for the practitioner, but it is not, mainly because the practitioner prepares for the session by practicing mental clearing techniques. These techniques help the practitioner achieve "hookup", in which energy - which Dr. Trager believed is all around us - flows through the practitioner to the client, facilitating the relaxation process.

The second component is called Mentastics and involves movement techniques, which the practitioner teaches the client to use on their own. In this way the relearning process begun in the tablework session can continue and the client can learn how to move without tensing up.

This course of study marked my official foray into the realm of neuromuscular rehabilitation, which has been my life's work for the past fifteen years, ever since retiring from drum and bugle corps in 1994.

* * *

News Flash!

We interrupt this dialog for an important bulletin!

Today, Friday, July 31st, 2009, is the DCI East Championships in Allentown, Pennsylvania. My son John is there in his role as brass caption head for the Concord Blue Devils. The corps is undefeated at this point in the season. They have just finished learning a new ending for the show, which they will debut tonight.

Chapter 26
1982 Dr. Frank Wilson

1982 was to be Jerry Seawright's last year as the director of the Blue Devils, and he tried his best to correct the "percussion problem" before handing over the reins.

He hired a percussion arranger/instructor who had been working with Spirit of Atlanta. Spirit's drum line had placed fourth in overall percussion, with a ninth place score in general effect, at the 1981 championship.

I distinctly recall my impressions at the time. I thought that Spirit's percussion writing came off as fast, flashy, and clean, but without the level of musicality and nuance that I had known in the writing of Rick Odello, Dennis Delucia, and Fred Sanford.

The Blue Devil staff was assured, however, that Terry Shalberg, who had been the percussion arranger for the Blue Devils since 1980, would still be writing the book.

Sad to say, that was not the way things worked out.

* * *

The opener for the 1982 season was a solid jazz number entitled *T. O.* by Rob McConnell and the Boss Brass. *Pegasus* was brought back from the 1980 show to fill the second production spot. The percussion solo was *Paradox* by Kansas. *One More Time Chuck Corea* was revamped from the '81 show, and the closer was *People Alone* by Lalo Schifrin.

It would prove to be a very cohesive show. It was very solid and extremely hot, and the sound of the brass once again sent me back to the drawing board. They were magnificent in every way. The contrabass section played with a new sense of power, warmth and presence, whereas the soprano section shined with a brilliance and clarity unmatched in my memory.

As a matter of fact, the show sparkled with soprano features. The soprano line had become the designers' darlings. They were featured both musically and visually throughout the show. You could always count on the soprano line to come through with a blowaway as long as they had the right material to work with.

An example of the right material to work with was the soprano feature in *T.O.* It was an articulative tongue twister and a flexibility nightmare. It demanded subtlety, range, power and stamina, but the performers loved it because it gave them the opportunity to show what they could do.

I don't think we lost a regular season show in 1982.

* * *

During that same year I met an extremely interesting man. His name was Dr. Frank Wilson, the father of Blue Devil baritone player Jeff Wilson. Dr. Wilson was a neurologist with the Kaiser Foundation, and he was intensely interested in how musicians do what they do. Needless to say, we had some great conversations.

One day I asked Frank his thoughts on the subject of evaluating tone quality. His thoughtful and amusing answer went something like this. Musical tone is a lot like great tomato soup; the only way to accurately define it is to taste it. And after you have experienced the taste of several different, great tomato soups, you learn how to evaluate tomato soup… tone quality.

Frank had a way of creating mental pictures to get you to see things in a different light. He would take an idea and look at it from various points of view, considering, evaluating, hypothesizing, until he would seemingly become bored with it and move on to another subject.

His mind was fast, very fast.

My mind, on the other hand was slow, very slow in comparison, but I thought it was great fun to follow him through his mental mazes and absorb as many concepts as I could, then attempt to sort them out at my leisure.

Dr. Wilson seemed most interested in the problem of focal dystonia, a situation whereby muscles no long function properly. These characteristic cramps or muscular contractions, which are usually brought on with task-oriented behaviors, can stop musicians in their tracks, leaving little hope for cure.

Frank Wilson would spend the next twenty years of his life in pursuit of the knowledge and understanding that was necessary to shed light upon both the cause and cure of this career-ending disorder.

* * *

News Flash!

The Blue Devils won the 2009 DCI East Championship last night with a 95.750.

As my son Tim would say, "so far so good."

* * *

By 1982 Edie and I and the boys had become nature lovers. We spent our vacations between Yosemite National Park and the beautiful Northern California Coast.

Edie was now a key figure in the commercial loan department for Bank of America Concord Main, and was spending time working with the C corps colorguard. Edie was also our vacation planner. She could always come up with a short weekend hop to any of a myriad of places, usually within a hundred and fifty miles of the Bay Area.

We accrued many great pictures and memories during those wonderful years when the boys were growing up. Edie and I worked hard to create a good life for us all. John was eleven years old, playing lead trumpet in the junior high band. He played first base in the JOBL junior baseball league, and solo soprano bugle in the C corps. He was actively involved in taking keyboard lessons on our new Yamaha Clavinova, and he was writing his own music, which at that time consisted mainly of rhythmic chord progressions, sparsely adorned with connective melodic figures.

Tim was seven years old and attending Meadow Homes Elementary School. He was the one and only screamer in the C corps with a double high C on a G bugle, written five ledger lines above the staff. Tim was not only a screamer, he was a true interpreter of the musical line; he took what you gave him and made it his own.

Tim was also getting into drawing at that time. He was always looking for something to draw. His most favorite images to capture on paper were TV wrestlers. He would draw them in action, in the ring, and believe me, he worked very hard on getting the perspective right.

1982 was a great year for me personally. The Blue Devils won their fourth high brass award and their third DCI World Championship in four years. We posted the highest score in DCI history - 95.250 - and from what I can recall, the corps went undefeated for the season.

Final breakdown of the scores placed The Blue Devils first in GE by one tenth over the Vanguard, first in brass by one point seven over the Vanguard, third in percussion by five tenths to the Bridgemen, and first in marching by two tenths over the Vanguard.

What I found truly amazing about all of this was that just four years before I had been testing out the effectiveness of my new bag of tricks, after a four-year layoff from teaching drum corps full time. I was the luckiest guy in the world for being in the right place at the right time, and I couldn't help wondering when it would all come to a screeching halt.

It was too good to be true.

Chapter 27
1983 Blue Devils - New Director

Each and every second of every single day is the most important moment of your life. It's the one and only moment when you're alive! It's the moment you've been waiting for to start enjoying life. The moment you have waited for so long. It's here! It's now! The moment of truth has arrived! Here comes the moment that oops! Just passed you by. There goes another one, and another, and another…

* * *

When you teach drum and bugle corps on a full time basis your vacation time comes after the DCI Championships, which are usually held in mid August. With the Blue Devils, the time off after DCI amounted to about two and a half months, give or take a few staff meetings and performances here and there.

For the three years previous to 1982 I had been using this "vacation" time to do research. One year I spent delving into the beauty and complexity of opera. I listened to arias, read librettos, followed scores, and read through critical commentaries. Another year I studied the music of Wagner, Berlioz, Nielsen, and Mahler. And yet another year I spent studying trumpet etudes and various forms of instructional brass literature.

But in the fall of 1982 I was hit with a creative streak that would manifest itself over the next twenty-seven years. I began writing. I began writing music.

I began writing lyrics, poems, and ideas. I wrote them down in notebooks, on scraps of paper, napkins, business cards, hotel memo pads, and on my new Mac computer. I would bring these ideas to my brother Tom who lived just a few blocks from our home in Concord. Tom played guitar and keyboards and had recently been studying the art of song writing.

I would go to Tom's house with a lyric and a melodic line and Tom would improvise a chord progression that set the proper mood for the piece. One song I remember quite well having created in this way was based on a poem I had written for my boys, John and Tim. It sounded like something Kermit the Frog might have sung, while sitting on a lotus blossom, basking in the sun. The lyrics went like this:

Life is a beautiful experience
Full of ups and downs it's true
But life is what you make it
Everything's left up to you
You can do anything you wish to do
You may choose to be sad or have fun
Just always remember that life is sweet
When you live it with love my son
Think only good and good things happen
Fill every day with joys dreams and memories
Give only love and you will be loved by everyone in return
When you dream a dream worth pursuing
One to challenge, demand and delight
Dream it again so you will remember it well
Cause dreams have a nice way of happening
When you just believe in yourself
Sample the gifts the world has to offer
Live your life fully gain wisdom with age
Endure pain and sorrow to kindle the fires of love
Sweet dreams, close your eyes
Daddy loves you my son

* * *

At any time of the day or night I could be struck by an incoming braistorm. I believed that if I wanted to encourage this flow of ideas I would have to honor the gift, which meant stopping whatever I was doing at the time to notate the thought, concept, revelation, or musical hook.

There were, of course, times when I did not stop what I was doing to notate the idea, but I found that the inspiration usually recycled through my awareness at a later date. I had no idea where these ideas were coming from, but I welcomed them into my life.

In order to create the time necessary for all of these brainstorming sessions I had to espouse a stronger awareness of the "kis" principle, which translates as keep it simple. In math I had always been interested in the lowest common denominator. I liked to break things down to their basic components, their elemental ingredients. Keeping things simple afforded me discretionary time to use as I saw fit.

* * *

Keep it simple, keep it simple, it's so much less confusing. Simplicity can bring clarity, and clarity is a rarity that could produce prosperity. When life is kept simple, there's lots of time for rest. There's time to improvise a lick and time to just be you. There's time for spontaneity, and levity, and brevity, and time for all those things you would truly love to do if only you had the time! Keep it simple.

* * *

1983 was a great year for the Blue Devil C corps. My son John and his good friend Mike Olivedas, who had begun his drum corps career in the C corps with John and Tim, were now out in front of the corps playing solos and duets on two-valve bugles just like the A corps. The C corps was becoming the talk of California drum corps.

The A corps was not faring as well. The directorship of the corps was changing hands. Jerry Seawright was doing his best to make a smooth, invisible transition but it was becoming clear, to me at least, that we would no longer have our class act at the helm. I could only hope for the best, but deep down I knew that the reasons I had come to the Blue Devils in the first place, the ideals and standards of a man like Jerry Seawright, were not going to be the order of the day from now on.

All things change, nothing remains the same…

One of my responsibilities since joining the Blue Devils in the fall of 1978 had been working the brass and percussion ensemble, which was a very satisfying situation until the 1982 season. The new percussion caption head was very difficult for me to deal with on a musical level. He wanted nothing to do with metronomes, consistent tempo, or musical interpretation. All he really wanted to do was win the high percussion award at DCI. I was never one to beat my head against the wall so I resigned my duties with the brass and percussion ensemble as of May 1983.

The show's opener in 1983 was a rehash of *T.O.* from the '82 season, with additional original music added on. That was followed by a hot arrangement of Maynard Ferguson's *Everybody Loves the Blues*. Next up was a repeat of the '82 drum solo *Paradox*, which led to yet another repeat of *One More Time Chuck Corea*, with additional original music added on. The closer was another piece of original music by the corps' arranger entitled *New Beginnings*.

All in all it was a most forgettable show, with the possible exception of Maynard Ferguson's *Everybody Loves The Blues*, which featured two wonderful soloists.

The big lesson I learned that year was that you can't create a great brass ensemble with a so-so musical book.

At finals we placed second in GE, third in brass, fourth in marching, first in percussion and second overall.

The 1983 DCI World Championship was won by the corps with the freshest concept in drum corps: The Garfield Cadets. The combination of George Zingali and Jim Prime was magical. Jim Prime's arrangements were smooth, musical, and professional, whereas George Zingali's drill designs were frenzied, mesmerizing, and pure genius. Together they expanded the drum corps envelope from letter size to legal.

Once again, drum corps had a new frontier to explore.

Chapter 28
1984 Blue Devils

Musical performance without artistry is like a cherry pie without the cherries: a hollow shell with no payoff.

Artistic musical performance is made possible by the natural human inclination toward inspiration and expression. Artistry demands imagination, originality and skill. It requires a free musical environment in which performers may learn to express their own special musical qualities and ideas.

This was the philosophy I aspired to during sectional rehearsals throughout the winter and spring of the 1984 season.

Instead of heading up the brass and percussion ensemble that year, I chose to spend my time in sectional rehearsals with the alto section, in addition to the sopranos and contrabasses.

Sectional rehearsals with all three sections were an absolute ball. With tunes like *Bacchanalia* by Steven Spiegl, *Latin Implosion* by Hank Levy, and *La Fiesta* by Chick Corea, sparks were guaranteed to fly at every rehearsal. We had the melody, counter melody and bass, and each part was Hot! Hot! Hot!

I would usually begin a sectional rehearsal by having everyone bop a particular section of music until it was light and clear. Then we might take one player on a part, or maybe just the sopranos and contras, or altos and sopranos, etc. until everyone felt comfortable. That was when we would put it all together and blow the roof off.

During these rehearsals I provided specific information when needed, but the basic overriding consideration was to make music and have fun with it. Eventually the performers realized what musical fun was all about: cooperating, supporting, leading, listening, reacting, responding, controlling and enjoying.

Oh, how Zen-like!

In 1984 the Blue Devil hornline consisted of a few high-powered four-year vets, a smattering of three-year vets, many two-year vets, and a large crop of solid rookies. The 1984 line would eventually become the strongest Blue Devil brass ensemble to date, and that was due, at least in part, to the fact that they had a great musical book to work with.

What more could a brass geek from the Bronx ask?

* * *

In 1983 my son John had moved up to the B corps with a group of his friends from C corps. The B corps was extremely fortunate to have a terrific brass instructor and arranger that year by the name of Dave Carico. Dave was a graduate of the Blue Devils and had been one of the fine baritone duet performers back in 1981. He was totally hyped about working with the B corps and did a great job of arranging, instructing, and motivating.

My son Tim took over the lead position in C corps when his brother John went to B corps. Tim loved playing his horn, and I must say he played it very well.

Tim has always been a natural, a born performer. Playing the bugle came easily for him, and perhaps because of that he demonstrated little desire to practice. He always knew his music because he could memorize so quickly, and his playing exhibited a sound that seemed to come from a vibrant energy source deep within him. I love the way Tim interprets music.

Both of my sons have always made me extremely proud. For them to be strong in what they feel is best for them, is what Edie and I support.

* * *

The new A corps director seemed to be more interested in gaining personal power and control than in promoting excellence and class. A kind of political hierarchy was permeating the workings and interrelationships of the Blue Devil staff. Whereas I had originally felt that a sense of anarchy reigned freely under Jerry Seawright's benevolent rule, the atmosphere around the staff these days felt more like a house divided against itself.

During the 1984 season the Blue Devils placed solidly in the top three spots at competitions across the country, but couldn't seem to get the show to jell. There were too many loose ends, too many places where things just didn't line up.

Of course there were always obstacles and differences of opinion to deal with during drum corps season, but in the end the idea was to fix problems so they went away for good, to allow the show to settle in. But in 1984 the brass and percussion caption heads were not willing to do what was necessary to fix and eliminate the timing, dynamic, and musical problems facing the brass and percussion performers.

We actually went into DCI final competition exhibiting the same balance, timing and interpretation problems that we had been experiencing in early season. These were problems that would have required, to one degree or another, a change in either the percussion or brass writing, but there was no course of action taken.

Where the drum corps was hurt most by this lack of action and initiative was not in the brass and percussion scores, but in the general effect scores. The musical ensemble did not communicate the show to the audience with a strong sense of unanimous musical intent.

Perhaps you remember the concept of locking together from the 1979 Whitewater show. Rock solid timing between musicians brings to music what a finely focused lens brings to visual image; it makes things clear and understandable. Clear musical presentation elevates the listener's ability to recognize and appreciate the more subtle aspects of musical performance. Truly great performers exhibit many personal characteristics but central to all great performances is supreme technical clarity.

* * *

News Flash!!!!

We interrupt this dialog for an instant news flash!

The Concord Blue Devils have just won the 2009 DCI World Class Championship in Indianapolis, Indiana with a score of 99.05 and the Concord Blue Devil B Corps has won the DCI Open Class Championship with a score of 95.5. Both Corps went undefeated for the entire season.

* * *

The 1984 DCI Championships were held in Atlanta, Georgia. Here is the rundown.

The Blue Devils placed second in GE brass by one tenth of a point, fourth in GE percussion by four tenths of a point, and second in GE marching by four tenths of a point. That added up to nine tenths of a point down to the first place Cadets in GE.

In brass execution there was a three-way tie for first place between the Cadets, the Blue Devils, and the Santa Clara Vanguard. The Blue Devils won percussion by nine tenths of a point over the Cadets, but lost marching to the Cadets by one tenth of a point.

We lost that championship by a mere one tenth of a point.

Chapter 29
Drum Corps Perspective

The 1980s were a great time to experience World Class Drum and Bugle Corps. New and innovative, or strongly traditional, it was all there, and it was being performed at the highest level of excellence drum corps had ever known. If you attended a DCI World Championship during the 1980s you saw a world-class event.

In 1985, the top ten corps competing for honors at the DCI Championships were the Troopers, Vanguard, Garfield Cadets, Blue Devils, Cavaliers, Phantom Regiment, Star of Indiana, Madison Scouts, Suncoast Sound, and Spirit of Atlanta. The evening's entertainment included music by George Gershwin, Gustav Holst, Leonard Bernstein, Aaron Copland, Emerson Lake and Palmer, Dmitri Shostakovich, Les Brown, Richard Strauss, and Hector Berlioz, plus a smattering of tunes from Walt Disney, and one complete show composed of original music.

Many of the people who worked on drum corps staffs in the 1980s had grown up in drum corps during the late 60s and 70s, and they wanted, just as I had, to add their mark to the ever-evolving activity we know as drum and bugle corps. They were talented, motivated young people who were ready to take a chance on something new and work to make it successful. They were innovators, motivators, teachers, musicians, and technicians, all with the same dream, and that was to create the best drum corps imaginable.

One such staff was that of the Santa Clara Vanguard. In my estimation theirs was the most musical brass and percussion ensemble on the field during the mid 1980's. The two people most responsible were Tim Salzman and Ralph Hardimon. Both of these men had the right idea when it came to musicianship and proper motivation. Ralph Hardimon had played and marched with drum corps in southern California and studied percussion with Fred Sanford in the early '70s, whereas Tim Salzman, a mid-west college band director, had been working with drum corps since the late '70s. Other members of the Vanguard musical staff had marched with the Santa Clara Vanguard, Concord Blue Devils, and Casper Troopers. But whatever their backgrounds, the Vanguard staff created a beautifully orchestrated blend of brass and percussion, complete with power, subtlety and nuance for all to enjoy.

* * *

Due to my responsibilities with the Blue Devil brass ensemble during pre-show warm-ups (fine-tuning, easing of physical and mental tensions, and stimulation of the initial adrenaline rush) I didn't have the opportunity to experience drum and bugle corps shows very often, but I still thoroughly enjoyed the activity.

Drum and bugle corps has something for everyone. Beyond performing, there are so many ways for a person to participate: as an instructor, board member, chaperone, cook, bus driver, or enthusiastic fan. Fans choose their favorite corps based on general effect, drill design, brass presentation, colorguard visuals, or percussion performance. Still other corps enthusiasts wholeheartedly support their own local drum and bugle corps.

As for me, drum corps allowed me to express myself, to explore my talents, to grow as a human being, and to give back to the activity that had given so much to me. Drum corps provided a consistent challenge for me to improve steadily from day to day. It endowed me with the habit of always moving forward in a positive direction, constantly reaching for the brass ring.

Chapter 30
1985 Blue Devils

The year was 1985. I was forty-three years old, my son John was fourteen, my son Tim was ten going on eleven and my wife Edie was beautiful going on gorgeous. I think I might have mentioned already that Edie has always had a beautiful posture, which I thought was related to her having been a Trooper. But as the years progress I see that her posture is a visual representation of her character.

Edie is a born leader, with a born leader's attitude; she expects events to go the way she plans them to go, and she projects an intention that simply makes it happen. Her manner is easy, slightly off-handed, definitely disarming. But above all, and certainly most important of all, Edie is a terrific mom. John and Tim must have done something very special in their past lives to have been given first pick when it came to moms.

John and Tim were now both in the Blue Devil B Corps. John had worked his way up in the hornline and was now out in front playing small ensemble features while Tim, in his second year of B corps, was playing lead soprano. Both of the boys fully enjoyed performing and rehearsing with the corps, and I was very pleased that they did. It had always been a dream of mine to offer them the same heartfelt emotional attachment to drum corps that I had experienced growing up in the Bronx.

* * *

I had been with the Blue Devils for six years at that point. In that time the corps had won three world championships and five high brass awards at DCI.

In 1985 we won our sixth high brass award in seven years.

The show that year was high energy all the way: *Life Raft Earth* by Darius Nordal, *Trilogy* and *Karn Evil 9* by Emerson Lake and Palmer, *Piano Concerto* by Keith Emerson, and *First Circle* by Pat Metheny. It was definitely the most difficult brass book I had ever taught. It demanded extreme amounts of heart, energy, and technical prowess from each and every brass performer. Every section of the brass line was challenged well beyond what I had ever experienced in drum corps before. The brass ensemble pulled off more of those hot, in your face licks, shouts, and full-blown choruses than any ensemble I had ever taught.

I salute and bow gracefully to the 1985 Blue Devil brass ensemble. They persevered through a season of instability. No matter what was asked of them they performed up to levels beyond my imagination.

The problem that year was once again due in large part to the disparity between brass and percussion performance techniques. There was a consistent lack of agreement between the two musical elements in regard to tempo, dynamics, and musical intent.

Once again, neither of the caption heads was willing to stand up and take responsibility for the ensemble's musical interpretation. It was a case of musical interpretation by committee, which of course never works, especially when the two people involved don't agree on basic musical concepts.

The corps was once again faced with the problem of the whole not being greater than the sum of its parts.

At the world championships that year the Blue Devils tied for high brass with the Garfield Cadets, took first place in percussion by a narrow margin, and took third place in marching by several tenths of a point. The big disparity once again was in general effect. We lost general effect by one point one, and lost the show to the Cadets by one point three, which put us in third place (by one tenth of a point) behind the Vanguard, who placed second.

It never bothered me to lose. What did bother me that year, though, was that the corps never achieved what they could have, or perhaps what they should have, based on the show's potential, the corps' talent, and the performers' willingness to work hard and always be at their best. Whereas Jerry Seawright had been expert in bringing people together to create something special, the new director of the Blue Devils did not seek or support cooperation with, or among, the staff. Without cooperation, nothing truly special was going to occur. What I witnessed from my perspective in the organization was the casual application of Machiavelli's precepts for gaining power: divide and conquer.

But things were about to take a decidedly different turn for the Blue Devil organization.

Chapter 31
Retro Show

Between the years of 1976 and 1982 the Blue Devil staff had fallen into a habit. To be more precise, they had developed a tantalizing taste for winning. During those seven years under the direction of Jerry Seawright they had won five world titles, and upwards of ninety percent of the competitions they had entered.

But during the ensuing years of 1983-85, without a man like Jerry Seawright to help guide them to victory, the staff's attempts to satisfy their taste for winning had been thwarted.

The meteoric rise of the Garfield Cadets did not help the Blue Devil cause any. In 1983 The Garfield Cadets became the new Cinderella corps, just as the Cavaliers, Troopers, Vanguard, Madison Scouts, and Blue Devils had been before them.

A Cinderella corps is one that comes along, resets the bar, and in some ways, redefines the activity. A Cinderella corps offers new dimensions in form, excellence, complexity, and nuance. The Garfield Cadets were all of that, and they were able to sustain that image through the years of 1983, '84, and '85.

* * *

During the waning months of 1985, however, there came forth a groundswell of enthusiasm within the Blue Devil organization. The drum corps was going to commemorate its first DCI win. This meant that the Blue Devils were going to play *Channel One Suite*, as performed by Buddy Rich, from the 1976 show, and the hot Latin production *Spanish Fantasy* by Chick Corea, from the 1978 show.

If I could have picked my favorite show of all time this would have been it. In every way this show fulfilled my vision of what a great horn-line needed to feast itself upon. Every section of the brass ensemble would have its day in the sun.

There were solos, section features, brassy shouts, and a sufficient number of "blow your face off" full ensemble statements to satisfy any insatiable drum corps fan. And perhaps the best part of the '76 retro show was that it was not the most difficult brass book I had ever taught, but it was the most enjoyable book I had ever taught.

There was one more special feature of the 1986 season, one that marked a milestone in my life. After six years of advancement through the Blue Devil C and B corps programs, my son John, at the age of fifteen, had become a lead soprano in the Blue Devil A corps.

We had about thirty rookies in the hornline that year, and as far as vets went, we had players with two, three, four, and five years of Blue Devil training and experience under their belts. You can bet that with four and five-year vets in the line we had leadership like never before. These were vets who were not going to be misled by a lack of unity among the staff. They knew what had to be done and nothing was going to stop them from doing it. Very early on in the season the members of the hornline demonstrated their intention to go all the way. They wanted nothing more to do with second and third place.

They wanted to be the best drum corps in the world!

At rehearsals I could feel them pushing me. I loved it because when they pushed me I pushed back. They played my exercises quicker, stronger, lighter, louder, softer and more articulately than I had ever imagined possible. They were happy to be doing what they were doing and they stood poised and ready for anything that came their way.

During rehearsals I could literally feel the force emanating from the hornline's strong intention to win. Their intention was tangible!

I have become convinced that a person's ability to establish and maintain a proper intention is the X factor when it comes to learning and performing. A clear intention facilitates physical movement and focuses the mind. A strong, singular intention coordinates the exclusive pattern of energy appropriate for the performance of the task at hand.

Picture a young college musician about to play an etude for his or her private teacher. An example of pure intention would be simply to make music, thereby creating a direct connection between intention and action: the intention to make music and the action of making music.

But let us say that in the student's previous lesson the teacher focused on minor mistakes and awarded a B for the effort. Because of this, the student might shift intention from making music to that of not making mistakes. This is an example of an ambiguous intention.

Not making mistakes has little to do with making music. In addition to being an ambiguous intention, not making mistakes also constitutes a negative direction. It is far better to aim at that which you wish to create (music) than it is to focus on that which you don't want to have happen (mistakes). The only proper intention when it comes to picking up a musical instrument and performing should be to make music.

* * *

In 1986, the Blue Devil brass ensemble wasn't the only section of the drum corps with a clear, strong intention, nor were they the only section of the corps that could claim a long list of vets. The colorguard boasted many veterans, some with up to sixteen years of competitive performance experience with the Blue Devil organization. The colorguard had more than its share of hard working, knowledgeable performers.

The percussion section, however, was composed primarily of rookies and second year veterans, but they too felt and identified with the intensity of willpower surging from both the brass ensemble and the colorguard.

As the season finally came upon us, it became quite clear to everyone on staff that we had a tiger by the tail, and that all we had to do was hold on tight and not let go.

Chapter 32
In The Zone

Ever since the first time I worked on Charlie Poole's hands in 1978 I have been using my hands to help others. I have always been glad to assist anyone who asked for help, and I can tell you for sure that people in drum corps are always in need of a little help.

During tour, the injured individuals came to me from the hornline, drumline, colorguard, and staff. They appeared out of nowhere during rehearsal, after rehearsal, before lights out, and first thing in the morning. As I said before, I loved doing the work, and it was a great way to practice my craft and get to know people I might otherwise not have had the opportunity to even talk to.

I also spent time on tour contemplating what I could do to help the brass performers be at their very best in competition.

Every little bit helped!

After long, hot, brass rehearsals I had the food crew put a bucket of ice out so the brass performers could cool their chops (lips) down. This helped with the problem of swollen lips.

Most nights after rehearsal I would distribute Jack's famous lip cream, which I made myself using a combination of vitamin E oil, lanolin, aloe gel, and peppermint oil. It served as a basic moisturizer and the peppermint oil added a cooling effect to relieve fatigue.

On tour I would cook dinner for the corps. Not every night mind you, but every once in a while, for special occasions. Before really big shows I would head to the food truck, and with the able assistance of the food crew, throw together a killer lasagna, or a spaghetti sauce to die for. It was a hype for the corps, it was a hype for the food crew, and it was a hype for me.

* * *

I have found over the years that being fully engaged in present moment activity calms and coordinates the human nervous system. Anything less than complete immersion in the present moment invites the possibility of mental distraction. Mental distraction disrupts concentration, which in turn suspends present moment awareness, resulting in a loss of mind/body coordination.

There are many ways to promote the habit of "being in the moment." Being in the moment is nothing more than not being in the past or future. The only possible way one can be in the past or future is in one's own mind. The practice of being in the moment promotes a clear, uncluttered mind. By definition, a clear mind is a mind at peace. Being in the moment and being at peace are therefore synonymous. In the next several paragraphs I offer a few of the practices that I used to promote being in the moment.

When I would call the hornline in from a rehearsal formation to talk to them, someone would invariably call out, "tell us a story, Uncle Jack." The Blue Devil hornline loved to have stories told to them. I am sure that they secretly enjoyed being transported to some magical place far from the day-to-day pressures of rehearsal.

One of my favorite books to read from was a book of Russian Folk Tales, which I had found in a small bookstore in Omaha, Nebraska one year while on tour. The book came complete with great illustrations of all the famous Russian folk characters like Baba Yaga and Koshchey the Deathless. I would read a story to them and at the proper time hold the book up so they could all see the picture, just like in kindergarten.

As the Blue Devil brass ensemble's biggest fan, I wanted them to be ready and able to give their all on the field of competition, and I knew that wasn't going to happen unless they felt at ease physically, mentally, and emotionally.

To wash away physical and mental fatigue we would stage water balloon relay races, or go on long nature walks, or sometimes the "kids" would simply enjoy running and jumping through a lightly wooded area, acting like dogs, monkeys, chickens, cows, or horses. The hornline worked extremely hard and I always thought they could use a little extra playtime to promote good mental health.

You can call it being in the moment or being in the zone, but the important thing to remember is that in order to improve your chances of being in that mode when the critical time comes you must practice "being there" on a regular basis.

The Blue Devil hornline knew how to practice. They practiced at being in the moment often enough to make it a very strong habit.

We are creatures of habit I've often heard said
But what exactly does that mean?
Does it mean we've no choice where habit is concerned?
Habits rule us completely?
Once a habit takes hold it stays until you're old?
I don't think we can put it that simply...
Habits are put in place by what we do over and over!
The care we take to do things just right
Fill all our moves with a grace and delight
To create such a habit you wouldn't believe?
Is a trick the best have hidden up their sleeve
Yes the best kind of habit is put in motion
With thought, intention and sometimes devotion
When it is time for the habit to function
It works like a charm! Smooth as silk! Not a hitch!
Habit takes over without missing a stitch

Chapter 33
1986 Early Season

The Blue Devils lost the first show of the 1986 season to the Santa Clara Vanguard by nine tenths of a point. People said that the reason they lost the show was that they were not in full uniform; they weren't wearing their spats. One week later, in Riverside, California, the Blue Devils managed to body slam the Santa Clara Vanguard by two full points. This time the corps was wearing their spats.

Throughout the California tour the Blue Devils remained undefeated in spats. They had begun the season in Sunnyvale, California with a score of 70.0. Twenty-eight days later on July 19th in Concord, California, the Blue Devils won the Drum Corps West Championship with a score of 89.2, to Santa Clara's 86.7.

The Blue Devils loaded up the caravan and left for Ogden, Utah that evening after the show. Nothing beats traveling down the road with a drum corps when everything is working the way it's supposed to. On the overnight drive to Ogden I recall stretching out on my bunk and giving some thought to my next brass rehearsal and how it would further my future goals. The rhythmic sounds of the motor and the light rocking of the bus helped to settle me down from the excitement and consequent reverie of the show earlier that evening.

I daydreamed a version of the next day's stretch and warm-up sequence. The stretching part of the rehearsal would have to take into account the long bus ride and lack of horizontal sleep. The warm-up would be aimed at pacing the performers to be mentally and physically ready to play full out by the end of the rehearsal block.

I typically chose a hyped section of the show to rehearse during the last fifteen minutes or so of a warm-up. In this particular case I chose the opening fanfare. First and last impressions are most important.

Our rehearsal in Ogden would be the first brass rehearsal of the 1986 DCI tour. I wanted it to be an indicator of great things to come. My aim was to create a dynamic sound bite for the introduction of the show. Jim Elvord had long ago taught me the value of using creative imagery to augment performers' understanding of what they were endeavoring to execute with great aplomb.

* * *

I remember waking to a morning mirage on the Bonneville Salt Flats just west of Salt Lake City. Luckily the air conditioner was working, but I could already feel the heat radiating from the window glass. I took the time remaining before our arrival in Ogden to write down a few notes about the rehearsal strategies for the day.

My plans for rehearsal were never carved in stone. I believed that it was best to be prepared, but open, ready to do the right thing when the situation presented itself. Always check the patient's pulse before deciding on the proper treatment.

* * *

We were situated atop a beautiful green knoll overlooking the school grounds in Ogden. To the east, as far as the eye could see, were the rugged mountains of the Wasatch-Cache National Forest. The temperature was warm, but not too warm, the air was clear, and for the most part it was quiet.

The stretch was slow and easy at first, but as everyone began to concentrate into the movements the intensity picked up. For the meditation I chose to introduce the concept of OM.

Om is not a word but rather an intonation, which, like music, transcends the barriers of age, race, culture and even species. It is made up of three Sanskrit letters, aa, au, and ma which, when combined together, make the sound Aum or Om. Om is a mantra or prayer in itself. If repeated with the correct intonation, it can resonate throughout the body so that the sound penetrates to the centre of one's being, the *atman* or soul.

Om is the sound of the universe. When pronounced, the sound forms just in front of the lips with A, moves smoothly into the mouth with U and is then swallowed with M.

* * *

And so it was that the Blue Devil hornline sat in a circle, in half lotus posture, for a time peacefully chanting the sound of the universe from atop the green grassy knoll in Ogden, Utah.

* * *

The brass rehearsal was reconvened in a shady spot, which promised a nice lively sound. Using the brick walls of the school as a backdrop the hornline set up a sectional arc, and we began warming up. During the breaks in the warm-up I went to each section in turn and delivered a dramatized scenario. This provided them with a mental image to help colorize their role in the fanfare. Along with this mental picture I imparted specific information about the total dynamic scheme and the part they played. By the end of the warm-up everybody knew the plan.

To execute the plan I asked for a totally integrated, three-dimensional arc. This meant contras evenly spaced throughout the arc, baritones evenly spaced throughout the arc, etc. etc. for each section. The low brass then moved four steps back, altos stayed where they were, and the sopranos moved four steps forward. This form provides its own resonance. It also emphasizes the bass voice, making it easy for the rest of the performers to feel their presence. To my ear it was the descending bass line that created the sense of depth and expansion for the show's opening.

It took ten minutes to get everything just right, but once accomplished the fanfare became alive, vibrant, and captivating. It was a big time blowaway! It was only forty counts long, but in forty counts the brass ensemble could have listeners down on their knees begging for more.

I cannot tell you what it was like to work with so many highly talented and motivated young people. Both then and now, the 1986 Blue Devil brass ensemble represents my overall favorite choice for ultimate hornline. It was truly a pleasure to be absolutely blown away day after day by their sound, their musicianship, their wholehearted participation, and their zest for life. I can only say thank you to each and every one of them for being there one hundred percent, and for making it possible for me to live my dream.

Chapter 34
1986 Finals Tour

The Blue Devils had been rehearsing extremely well since their arrival in Ogden, Utah just four days before. So well, in fact, that the staff decided to give them the afternoon off at a local bowling alley on the day of the Denver show. There is something deeply satisfying about throwing a bowling ball down an alley and blasting ten exposed, defenseless pins in all directions while shootin' the breeze with your friends. The "kids" were fully alive and in the moment!

With an afternoon of bowling, dinner, show preparation, and bus loading under their belts, the corps was free of frustration and riding high as they headed down Interstate 25 toward Mile High Stadium.

As the caravan rounded the last bend before the stadium exit, the lights, the field, and the capacity crowd rolled slowly and dramatically into view. It was truly a spectacular sight.

The Blue Devil buses started rocking!

That night during the show I stood on the track at Mile High Stadium talking with Mr. Jones about his favorite topic; caption scores, rankings, and overall ratings. Mr. Jones loved competition, and to him it was all about the numbers. When he looked at the scores, his first thought was about how he could improve the number. And of course Jim Jones knew exactly what had to be done... rehearse, rehearse, rehearse!

When I told Mr. Jones that my son John was playing lead soprano in the Blue Devils, his face lit up with his famous gentleman Jim smile, and I caught just a hint of nostalgia in his eye as he nodded his heartfelt joy for me. Then we went back to talking about drum corps: equipment trucks, scores, and tour logistics. Some things never change.

I had the opportunity that evening to view the show from the front row of the upper deck. A huge full moon filled the eastern sky, which served as a storybook backdrop for the Denver show. The Blue Devils presentation was far and away the best drum corps performance I had ever experienced at Mile High Stadium. It was the stuff from which legends are made. The corps blasted through the ninety barrier with a total score of 94.4, four and a half points above the corps' previous score.

The Blue Devil tiger was roaring and we were all holding on for dear life.

From Denver, the Blue Devils went northeast and Santa Clara headed southeast. Santa Clara's record with the Blue Devils up until that point had been 1 first place and 12 second places, and the Blue Devils' record was 1 second place and 12 first places.

As the two corps progressed across the country they each won decisive victories in all of their respective competitions. Santa Clara and the Blue Devils met up once again, eleven days later, on August 6th in Huntington, West Virginia.

I had the opportunity to view both corps' performances that evening from about half way up the stands and I could not pick a winner. Three nights before, Santa Clara had scored a 93.4 and the Blue Devils a 93.8 in their respective shows. The night before the Huntington show Santa Clara's score rose to a 93.7 in Sevierville, Tennessee. So there was no doubt that the two corps were neck and neck.

After all was said and done in Huntington, the Blue Devils remained undefeated in spats. The respective scores were 94.4 and 94.8.

On August 7th, the night after the Huntington show, the Blue Devils scored another 94.8 in Evansville, Indiana, and Santa Clara scored a 95.2 in Cincinnati, Ohio... Hmmmmm.

This was when the Blue Devil staff spread the word that DCI was now in the business of selling tickets to the final showdown.

(In 1986, drum corps recap sheets were hotter than tomorrow's news. Everyone knew instantly what was happening in other shows around the country. The duel between Santa Clara and the Blue Devils became widely known throughout the drum corps activity. A dramatic competition between two neck and neck rival corps would help to fill the stadium in Madison, Wisconsin for the World Championships.)

On August 9th in Whitewater, Wisconsin the Blue Devils scored a

94.4, but in Marion, Ohio, Santa Clara posted a 95.4.

Oh, they were really selling tickets now!

I was beginning to feel like I was in a horse race, but that I was fading back and there was nothing I could do about it. The horse I was racing against was running on another track, in another state.

On August 10th, in Stillwater, Minnesota (the Blue Devils second home) the corps scored a 95.4, while in Port Huron, Michigan, Santa Clara's score went down to a 94.0.

The next day on August 11th the Blue Devils broke through to a 96.3 in Minneapolis, Minnesota, and Santa Clara jumped to a 96.2 in Rockford, Illinois. The number race between the two corps could not have been more incredible if it had been scripted by a DCI executive.

* * *

The Blue Devils knew how to prepare for world championship competition. The strategy was to work hard on Monday, Tuesday, and Wednesday of championship week, which meant full twelve-hour rehearsal days. The only exception was that on Wednesday morning those who had signed up for the individual and ensemble contest, plus anyone who wished to go to root them on, went to the competition.

In order to have the performers at their very best for the preliminary competition on Friday night the corps was allowed to sleep in a bit on Thursday morning, and even longer on Friday morning, so they would have that much more energy for the Friday night show.

The last run through on Thursday night was timed to occur at exactly the same time as the corps would perform in the preliminary competition on Friday night, which was at about ten o'clock.

Thursday night's run-through, performed in half uniform, was the best of the year.

The next night, Friday night, at the DCI preliminary competition, the corps pulled off their best performance of the year to date.

But there was no doubt in my mind that each individual had yet another level of performance to achieve, like a rose that has not yet reached the zenith of its bloom, but stands imminently poised on the brink of final maturation.

The next morning I met the hornline outside of the school at eleven o'clock.

It was finals day!

The corps had been treated to a leisurely morning with both wakeup, and breakfast, as you like it. We were about to embark on our last nature walk to find a memorable warm-up spot.

About a ten-minute walk down a country lane I had scouted out a nice, quiet location, complete with a lake, which is not unusual in Wisconsin, and lots of tall trees, surrounding an open area large enough for our needs.

The hornline was in great spirits. This was the last day these performers would ever spend together as an ensemble. They knew very well that when they woke the next morning it would be all over, gone. They were out to make the best of the time they had left together.

With their instruments in tow they headed off down the lane chanting a selection from the Vanguard '86 repertoire, *The Hut* from Mussorgsky's Pictures at an Exhibition. *The Hut* refers to Baba Yaga's hut, which stands on chicken legs and turns round and round in a clearing in the forest: it is a very agitated, in your face kind of melody.

As we made our way down the road to the lake I became aware of the fact that I was literally having the time of my life. Teaching drum corps was a good thing for me to be doing.

We were in Wisconsin in August. It was a warm, humid day with a slight, but refreshing breeze coming in off the water. Upon arriving at our destination we went immediately into our 'first warm-up of the day' routine. I had the hornline all to myself for two hours.

It was a total thrill to have such a fine brass ensemble to work with, especially when they were at the top of their game, as they were that morning. My aim was to complete the metamorphosis we had begun back in January. Just as in the story of Pinocchio when the wooden-headed puppet is transformed into a real live boy, I was hoping to complete the brass ensemble's musical journey by stimulating their natural propensity for self-expression. The performers knew and understood the musical dynamics of the show. My job was to encourage an even stronger sense of confidence in themselves and in each other, and to take that final step toward free musical expression.

The first part of the warm-up was done with virtually no verbal communication. This was my way of pushing the performers to use their wits, to interpret my visual cues, which they did to perfection. Through subtle movements of my hands they interpreted and expressed musical nuance. They were right where they needed to be: in the moment, in the groove, in the zone, one hundred percent in the here and now.

After the warm-up, which lasted about fifteen minutes and was composed mainly of long, lovely tones with slurs, pedals, and chords, we did a leisurely stretch in the little clearing, beneath the trees, by the lake.

The final part of the stretch sequence was devoted to sense awareness. While lying on their backs, each individual would notice the closest sound, the farthest sound, the softest sound, the loudest sound; the warmth of the sun on their bodies or the texture of the earth beneath them; the many scents in the air, the beat of their heart, and the varied visual patterns of tree and sky.

This was the basic practice of simply being, becoming present and aware.

"Yesterday is history. Tomorrow is a mystery. And today? Today is a gift. That's why we call it the present."
Babatunde Olatunji

"The ability to be in the present moment is a major component of mental wellness."
Abraham Maslow

While present and aware, everyone gathered around to hear the tale of *Finist The Bright Falcon*. I chose this particular tale because of the fierce determination exhibited by the heroine to accomplish her goal of finding and reuniting with her Love, who had cried out to her in her sleep, "If you want me, you must walk to the other end of the earth, beyond the thrice-ninth land to the thrice-tenth kingdom. Before you find me, you'll wear out three iron staffs, tread down three pairs of iron shoes, and swallow three stone loaves."

Another reason for choosing this story was that it had many repeated sections like, "Foo, foo, foo!" snorted Baba-Yaga. "In the old days you never so much as glimpsed a Russian soul in these parts. Now I can see them and hear them and smell them and they even walk into my hut," which I had hoped everyone would pick up on, and they did. It was a little like being at a cult movie where everyone knows and recites the key phrases throughout the story.

My personal favorite of these repeated phrases occurs when the heroine first discovers Baba-Yaga's hut, which stands on chicken legs turning round and round in circles.

"Stay still little hut. Turn your back to the forest and your door towards me. I'm hungry. I want to come in." The hut spun round till its door was right in front of her. She went in. There on the floor lay Baba-Yaga. Her bony legs stretched right to the far corner. Her lips rested on a shelf on the wall. Her nose almost touched the ceiling.

They enjoyed the story. From the story we moved into a full half hour warm-up, which crescendoed into more rousing fun than anyone should be allowed to experience without goose bump protectors.

* * *

The Blue Devils swept all captions that night. High brass, high percussion, high marching, and high general effect, with a score of 98.4 to Santa Clara's score of 97.0. That made the seventh high brass award the Blue Devils had received during the eight years I'd spent with the corps.

Chapter 35
Jim Jones - Perspective

1986 marked Jim Jones' last year as director of the Casper Troopers. For thirty years he had devoted his time, talents, and energy to create and establish the Troopers for the young people of Casper, Wyoming to experience. During those many years he touched the lives of thousands of people, many of whom he had never met. Consider how the world of drum corps, and the lives of thousands of people, might have been changed had Jim Jones never created the Casper Troopers.

The inspirational film *It's a Wonderful Life*, starring Jimmy Stewart, tells the story of a man who is magically afforded the opportunity to experience, first hand, how people's lives would have been negatively transformed had he never been born. The film demonstrates in dramatic fashion how we all affect each other's lives, and how personal interactions influence the very fabric of community living.

Every day we touch the lives of others, sending energy and reverberations far into the future, affecting people we may never meet. The idea of completely erasing a single individual's life and social influence from the continuum of time is both far-reaching and mind-boggling.

Two lives that were directly and deeply affected by Jim Jones' actions were those of my wife Edie and myself. Unlike in the film, Edie and I will never have the opportunity to see what might have been if Jim Jones and the Troopers had never existed. But we are pretty sure of what would never have happened.

For one thing, I would not be writing this memoir. Chances are Edie and I would never have met, we would never have married, and our son John would not be teaching the Blue Devils.

The chances are good that there would be no Blue Devils, because Fred Sanford and Pete Emmons would never have gone to California in 1965, offering the knowledge they had gained from the Troopers, to beginning drum corps like the Anaheim Kingsmen and the Santa Clara Vanguard. The brilliant success of these two drum corps, as well as the colorful mystique of the Casper Troopers, must have provided the motivation needed to inspire Jerry Seawright to establish the Blue Devils drum and bugle corps in the first place back in 1972.

Jim Jones pioneered the concept of the touring drum corps purely out of necessity, and he was perfectly willing to share the information he had gathered over the years with other drum corps directors. This was particularly true of Mr. Jones' desire to assist the west coast corps in their pursuit of full out, nation wide touring.

In 1967, ten years after Jim Jones had started the Troopers, and one year after the Troopers had won their first VFW title, the Anaheim Kingsmen took a ten-day tour to the VFW National Competition in New Orleans and placed 13th in the preliminary round.

In 1969, the Santa Clara Vanguard toured all the way to Boston, and amazingly made it back home again after having placed 13th at the VFW National Competition in Philadelphia.

In 1970 Santa Clara won the American Legion National title and the North American Open title, beating the Casper Troopers for the very first time.

In 1971 the Vanguard won the VFW national title with the Troopers, 27th Lancers, Blue Rock, and Anaheim Kingsmen completing the top five.

In 1972, the first year of DCI competition, the Blue Stars, Madison Scouts, and Casper Troopers all went west for the first time ever to compete in a series of shows in sunny California.

In that same year of 1972 the Anaheim Kingsmen won the first DCI World Championship in Whitewater, Wisconsin with the Blue Stars, 27th Lancers, Vanguard, and Argonne Rebels completing the top five.

From 1972 onward to the year 2010 well over half of the DCI World Championships have been won by California drum corps.

Today, all highly competitive drum corps go on extensive tours, but that was not the case in 1965. In those days the midwest and east coast drum corps competed mainly at "local" shows on weekends, and finished off the season with an excursion to the VFW or American Legion national competitions in August. But by the mid 1970s, touring drum corps had become the rule, not the exception, in this highly competitive arena.

Chapter 36
1987 Bollinger Canyon

If I knew then, what I know now, things would have been so much easier, so much less confusing. But then, I suppose stumbling around in the dark was somehow necessary for me to learn what I now know. Something as simple as sitting quietly, surrounded by the nature of things, with a clear non-striving mind, was not in my vocabulary.

I was always thinking ahead. I was picturing and planning the future, my future, our future. And when the future came into being, I was busy planning the new future, which was all well and good, but I wasn't making the pilgrimage to the top of the mountain often enough to observe life from a distance. I was not taking the time to restore my life energies to the bottom line. Like the little train chugging up the hill, I just kept pushing.

So when I returned from tour in 1986 I set my mind on a new goal. I wanted to design a new alto instrument. I went to Zig Kanstul and explained my idea. My reason for wanting a new alto horn was that I wanted to have one type of alto instrument instead of three in the brass ensemble. We had been using French horns, flugelhorns, and mellophones in the alto section, and while the sound was solid, it was also a little thick and heavy. It lacked clarity, especially when split into six parts. I wanted a lyrical quality, with a clean, clear, alto timbre.

When I explained the instrument that I had in mind to Zig Kanstul, he told me that what I had described was a descant French horn. When I asked Zig if he could build one he said he had no idea if it were possible, but that he would try.

I was modeling the new alto instrument after the old Conn French horn bugle from the fifties, which had a long gracefully tapered bell with a slight flare at the end. (The flare at the edge of a brass bell emphasizes high overtones, like the pancake flare of a mellophone bell, which gives the horn its distinctive tone.)

The instrument that Zig made for me was basically a long, tapered bell with a set of valves. It had a very short leadpipe that entered directly into the first of the two valves. The rest of the horn was all bell: long and graceful, with no flare.

The tuning slide was in the leadpipe where the mouthpiece enters the horn. I chose a special flugelhorn mouthpiece to properly augment the sound of the instrument. It was truly a beautiful horn, but it had one monumental flaw. It possessed only one usable octave; from second line G to top space G. Everything else was unplayable. It had a clear, strong, lyrical quality and the sound was so good that we decided to go with it.

Zig christened the new horn the Meehaphone, which I guess he figured was better than the Zigaphone or the Jackhorn, and built fourteen of them for the Blue Devils.

* * *

Near the end of 1986, California experienced what came to be known as the Indian bingo scare. The management of the Blue Devils feared the worst for their bingo game and began cutting expenses. I was told by the A corps director that my job description was going to change and that I would be free of my responsibilities with B and C corps.

I thought it best to diversify!

I took the appropriate tests to obtain a state teaching credential and upon passing the CBEST test with flying colors I was hired on by the San Ramon Valley Unified School District.

I enjoyed the work I had done with the Blue Devil B and C corps and decided that it might be fun to take on an elementary school music program. The school district had an immediate opening at the Bollinger Canyon Elementary School.

The school was beautifully situated at the entrance to Bollinger Canyon, a few blocks west of interstate 680. The principal, whose name was Joan Diamond, was a real gem. She cared deeply about the kids and wanted the best for them. And on top of that, she was a people person; she knew how to get what she wanted for the kids without alienating the staff.

On the first day that I reported for duty, I was informed that the last music teacher at Bollinger Canyon was not very enthusiastic and that there were only three students in the music program. After meeting with the students I decided to begin preparations immediately for a Christmas Concert. It was already November. We would have a good six weeks to get ready.

I had the students bring in recordings of their favorite songs. I took the recordings home and used a four-track Tascam porta-studio to create backup arrangements, which were performed on a Yamaha CVP6. I also confiscated a huge loudspeaker-amp combination so the kids could get the feel of being backed up by a big band.

Each of my three young musicians received a cassette recording of the arrangements and a computer generated part for them to read, so they could learn to play along with the "band in the box." It was like music minus one, or instrumental karaoke if you like. They each had two solos with band accompaniment and they each took part in a trio of trios, which were also complete with band accompaniment.

The Christmas program was a complete success. The three young performers became famous among their peers, and the concert helped to raise the number of students participating in the music program from three to forty-two for the spring semester.

I expanded my audio-assist program by creating arrangements to go along with the instrumental music series I was using with the students. By using the band in the box I didn't have to struggle to keep the young musicians playing together. This allowed me to spend my time going from individual to individual making corrections in posture and body mechanics.

 Meanwhile, the kids were learning to maintain a steady tempo, and their listening was naturally gravitating toward the pitch of the sounds emanating from the speaker box. I had arranged a short introduction for the beginning of each of the tunes so as to attract the students' musical attention to the tonality and tempo of the recorded accompaniment.

In the six years I taught at Bollinger Canyon Elementary School, the music program swelled from three students in November of 1986 to almost three hundred students in June of 1992.

Chapter 37
1987 Season and Judging Perspective

Teaching world class drum and bugle corps was a challenge. Each and every year was a learning experience. In 1987 I had the opportunity to learn again what it was like to start over. The 1986 Blue Devil hornline had been the result of four years of hard work. I had gained a wealth of knowledge, wisdom, and understanding from the experience, but now I was faced with the task of instilling that knowledge and understanding, as quickly as possible, into the operational psyche of a rookie brass section.

I immediately set out to compose several original pieces of music. My idea was to raise the performers' level of awareness in the area of melodic interpretation and phrasing. And going hand and hand with this idea was the new alto horn that Zig Kanstul had designed for us. I was hoping to create a new sound that would prove to be more lyrical, but at the same time potently powerful.

For the opener and second production of the show that year I suggested two tunes that I had always wanted to teach and perform. They were both wonderfully melodic in nature. One was *Fanfare for the New*, by Hugo Montenegro (performed by Stan Kenton's Neophonic Orchestra) and the other was *Harlem Nocturne*, by Earle Hagen and Dick Rogers.

When Jerry Seawright was the Blue Devils director, no single individual had the final say when it came to choosing the musical selections for the show. It was up to the whole staff to choose music that everyone felt positive and comfortable with. But all that changed when Jerry resigned as director of the corps in 1983. Under the new order of things, the corps director decided to claim the final say for himself, and in doing so, succeeded in alienating various factions of the staff.

That was the case once again in 1987. The A corps director chose *Fanfare for the New* and *Harlem Nocturne* to be used in the 1987 competitive show, but there was strong dissent from the percussion staff about those choices. The concerns of the dissenting staff members were brushed aside, eventually leading to a breakdown in open communication among the staff, and to a myriad of production problems during the competitive season.

The rest of the 1987 program included *Enchinadas Arf* (Frank Zappa), *Free* (Chicago), and *Spanish Dreams* (Doc Severensen). All in all it was a good show, although not a winner, primarily because the second half of the show, which consisted mostly of rehashed material, paled in comparison to the innovative music and arrangements of the first half.

It was, however, a good solid program for our young hornline to gnaw away on, and it was jam packed with stylish melodic lines, making it a perfect vehicle to support the musical direction I had decided to take toward my next ultimate hornline (the sequel). As things eventually turned out, I was only going to be given one more opportunity to create something really special with the Blue Devil brass ensemble.

In 1986 I had learned just how strongly performer attitude affected the final outcome of the season. When the '86 Blue Devil brass ensemble had been in rehearsal, their main aim, their fullest intention, was to blow the staff away. They wanted to silence the critics. They wanted to stimulate positive commentary. (They probably wanted get out of rehearsal early so they could get some well-deserved rest). And the only way they could make that happen was to consistently perform better than ever before.

Every rehearsal was a performance. Every time the horn came up provided another opportunity to improve. That was their attitude! That was their MO. That was what drove them to become one of the finest drum and bugle corps of all time. They truly wanted to make their mark in the annals of drum corps, and they'd possessed, in spades, the internal leadership to make it happen. Believe me, it was really tough to see that wonderfully talented group of performers age out.

But by 1987, the C and B corps programs really started to pay off. I had a rookie A corps brass section but it was peppered with a few notable exceptions. Several of the key players in the line had been per-forming with the Blue Devil organization since they'd joined C corps in 1980, and they knew my rehearsal expectations like they knew the back of their hand: pay close attention, work hard, improve daily, and have a good time doing it. Unlike other rookie hornlines that I had taught in the past, this one had a solid core of young leaders who led the way at every rehearsal.

* * *

1987 was a rebuilding year for the Blue Devil hornline. Seventy-five percent of the soprano section and sixty percent of the alto section were rookies. The contrabass section averaged out at about two years of Blue Devil experience, and fifty percent of the baritones were rookies.

My son John became the featured soloist, soprano section leader, and one of the most influential personalities in the brass ensemble. The leadership role was not a new one for John since he had taken on the same function and responsibilities in both the B corps and the C corps.

My son Tim decided not to march in 1987 because at twelve years old he was too young to try out for the A corps and the ranks of the B corps had been decimated due to decisions being made by the A corps director. So instead of marching drum corps that year, Tim was going to spend his summer with his cousin Josh in the small mining town of Dillon, Colorado, just west of Denver.

* * *

The 1987 competitive season played out like a bad case of reverse deja vu when compared to what had occurred in 1986. The Santa Clara Vanguard won every show in California! The Blue Devils didn't even get to win the first one (as Santa Clara had the year before). By the time we got to Denver we were ready to go our separate way from the Vanguard. That year, Santa Clara was heading north and east, while we were going south… and eventually east. The Blue Devils won eight of their next eleven shows going into championship week. Santa Clara was undefeated going into championship week. DCI was being held, once again, in Madison, Wisconsin.

(Something to remember: as of 1987, eleven of the fifteen DCI world championships had been won by California drum corps. The exceptions were Madison Scouts in 1975 and the Garfield Cadets in '83, '84, and '85. I can only imagine that the midwest based DCI organization was not too happy about the twelve year drought for its midwest corps, and certainly no one in the DCI front office wanted a California corps to win yet another DCI title.)

Let's look at the results of the preliminary and final rounds of the 1987 DCI World competition.

This is what happened in the preliminary competition.

In fifth place with a score of 93.900... The Cavaliers!
In fourth place with a score of 95.000... The Blue Devils
In third place with a score of 95.600... Phantom Regiment
In second place with a score of 96.500... Santa Clara Vanguard
And in first place with a score of 97.000... The Garfield Cadets

During the preliminary competition, the scores were posted as soon as they were tabulated, so everyone in the stands knew the score for each of the corps soon after their performance. It was always a great time for "ooos and ahhhs" as the scores were metered out between performances to the anxiously awaiting fans. But the ovation produced by the crowd when the announcement of Santa Clara's score resounded through the stadium struck me as an extremely loud mixture of "boos and cheers." It was obvious that there was a healthy mix of extremely vocal fans in the audience that night.

The Vanguard and the Cadets had met four times during the regular season before appearing in the world championship preliminary competition. At the DCI East show in Allentown, the Vanguard won over the Cadets by one point four. In Garfield, New Jersey, the Vanguard won by one point two. At the West Chester show the difference had dwindled to only three tenths of a point in favor of the Vanguard. But at the Saint Louis show, Santa Clara had bested the Cadets one more time by the sizable spread of one point two.

They were both very fine drum corps!

The Vanguard's show tended more toward the traditional side, with a very high degree of excellence in all captions. The theme was Russian, with music by Mussorgsky and Khachaturian. The colorguard was dressed as Cossacks and Russian peasant girls. The brass and percussion performers wore Russian headgear, and the show ended with a Russian style magic trick, performed to the grandiose sounds of *The Great Gate of Kiev*. It was really a fine production.

The Cadets' show was as uniformly thematic as you can get. The entire show was composed of one piece of music, beautifully arranged by Michael Klesch: *Appalachian Spring* by Aaron Copland. It was not a traditional style drum corps show, but it was vintage Cadets, featuring the inspired visual designs of the genius from Revere, George Zingali.

This was how the final competition played out.

High general effect brass... Vanguard by one tenth
High general effect percussion... Cadets by three tenths
High general effect visual... Vanguard by six tenths
High brass performance... Cadets and Vanguard tie
High visual performance... Cadets and Vanguard tie

(So far the Santa Clara Vanguard was ahead by four tenths of a point and neither the brass judge nor the visual judge had performed their main function: to rank the corps. As far as any dyed in the wool drum corps person would be concerned, a tie is a copout!)

High percussion performance... The Cadets by five tenths

The Cadets, the corps with the most thematic production that didn't hail from California, won the fifteenth DCI Championship by one tenth of a point over that season's top performer, the Santa Clara Vanguard. The brass and visual performance judges did not do their job. Instead they left it up to the percussion performance judge, who was apparently more than eager to have his say.

The Blue Devils finished fourth overall.

* * *

Before the 1980s, drum corps competition had always been strongly aimed at determining which competitive unit was the absolute best. It had been decided that a preliminary round and a final round would be necessary to decide the winner in national competition. The reason for this was obvious: if you wish to determine the very best drum corps, you must first employ a process of elimination by ranking and rating the participants in a preliminary round of competition, and then have them perform in reverse order of finish for the final round. This allows for a more precise system of comparison and adjudication.

Fierce competition had always been the motivating stimulus that spearheaded the rise of drum and bugle corps from its lowly position in the world of musical pageantry in the early '50s, to the world-renowned status that it enjoyed in the '80s. The pioneers of drum corps were competitors in the truest sense of the word. They were all vying for the top prize. They each wanted to be the best.

Drum corps competitions and band competitions are not the same. In a typical band competition units are rated, but not necessarily ranked. In a drum corps competition, it is the judge's primary job to decisively rank the competitive units (first, second, third) and then as accurately as possible, rate their performances (numerical score) based on specific criteria.

Judges who adjudicated drum corps competitions in the 50s, 60s, and 70s, were for the most part dyed in the wool drum corps people. They understood the importance of accurately ranking and rating the participants. The excellence that drum and bugle corps had achieved through this rigorous adjudication style attracted many interested professionals from high school and college music programs and by the early '80s, these band people, who were not dyed in the wool drum corps people, were integrating into the drum corps judging profession.

Along with this influx of non-drum corps judges, the traditional tic system of judging had recently been replaced by a more subjective system of evaluation, which relied principally on opinion (hopefully professional opinion as opposed to personal opinion). Though subjectivity was not supposed to replace objectivity, in practice, it did. Systematic ranking and rating became defused. Personal opinion and preference became the order of the day. It had become more important to supply judges with an integrated theme for a show than it was to display traditional high-energy drum corps style excellence. The fierce, competitive nature of drum and bugle corps was slowly being eroded through the diluting effects of outside interests and concerns.

Chapter 38
1988 John and the Blue Devil Show

One morning, while on tour in 1987, I happened to be sitting in a stadium, half way up the lower deck at about the thirty-yard line. I was observing how the Blue Devil hornline reacted and responded to the instructions given by the visual staff during a marching rehearsal. What I found intriguing was that when the hornline was permitted a break, a clot of people would form around my son John, wherever he happened to be on the field. I had my trusty notebook and pencil with me, so I spent some time in the warm morning sun writing down these heartfelt lines about my wonderful son John.

> He's a brilliant shining moment in the history of my life
> The symbol of love between a husband and wife
> With a heart as big as all outdoors and bright as he can be
> He's the perfect blend of common sense and sensitivity
> He radiates self-confidence, he is wise beyond his years
> He is everything a son could be, a prince among his peers
> A man of sturdy principles, he will always treat you right
> And he lights up like a Christmas tree on competition night

John was going into his ninth year of performing with the Blue Devils. It was his third year in A corps. Tim auditioned in November of 1987 for the A corps hornline and was accepted at the tender age of thirteen. Believe it or not, 1988 marked Tim's eighth year of playing lead soprano in the Blue Devil organization.

* * *

The musical repertoire for the 1988 show fit the Blue Devils brass ensemble like a newly tailored suit of clothes. It was hip, savvy, crisp, elegant, and sophisticated, and it showcased the finest collection of soloists ever to grace the field of competition. *Happy Days Are Here Again* (Barbra Streisand), *That Old Black Magic* (Ashley Alexander), *Goodbye Yesterday* (Buddy Rich), and *Since I Fell For You* (Bob James), went together like bacon and eggs, corned beef and cabbage, Bogart and Bacall. The show was a musical tour de force, with a little something for everyone. As for me, it was exactly what I needed to finely hone my lyrical brass fantasy hornline into shape. The 1988 show was destined to become a melodic masterpiece.

Once again, I was working with the sopranos, altos, and contrabasses in sectionals. All in all, sectional rehearsals were a joy. The soprano parts offered every style of melodic line imaginable, the altos were given intricate and soaring counter-melodic lines to play, and the contrabasses wove it all together with long, graceful, melodic phrases creating a tapestry of colorful brass counterpoint, inspiring stylish musical performance.

I learned a few very interesting things in 1988. I was able to grow as a musician because I was being faced with new challenges. Along with the more lyrical style of music came a far greater need for inspired phrasing. It takes more than a great tone and the right notes to really sell a melodic line. Melodic phrasing demands the subtle use of dynamic shadings, and a gig bag full of stylistic articulations.

But being that this was drum corps, it was necessary to wield these subtle nuances at the fullest spectrum of volume. The performers soon discovered that it took a fantastic amount of energy to perform in this extreme musical manner. It was mentally and physically draining, so much so that I found it essential to pay special attention to the performers' energy levels during rehearsal, to keep from over-taxing their physical and mental endurance. I could usually tell if they needed a break by either looking into their eyes or observing their 'at ease' postures.

Rehearsing performers when energy levels are low brings about poor performance habits!

Throughout the winter and spring of '88, the Blue Devil brass ensemble explored, in great detail, the varied textures and gradations of the forte volume range, from the softest mezzo forte to the loudest for-tissimo. Dynamics were utilized to shape and enhance every phrase of music. If a musical line ascended or descended in pitch, there was a corresponding dynamic dimension added to enhance the phrase. No dynamic nuance was left unresolved. Every aspect of every phrase was adorned with loving attention.

One of the most important aspects of the whole process for me, though, was that my two sons, John and Tim, were right there to explore it all with us.

* * *

It's funny how isolated rehearsals from over twenty years ago stand out with crystal clarity in my memory. I am recalling one such day in May of 1988. It was a camp weekend, and it was held at James Logan High School, located in Union City, California. The two main thrusts of the Saturday rehearsal were to put the opener drill (*Black Magic*) on the field, and to solidify the closer (*Since I Fell For You*) with the brass ensemble.

I remember feeling absolutely thrilled the first time I heard and saw the opener production being put together on the field. The movements of the drill beautifully complemented the activity and drive of the music. All of the voices were wonderfully exposed and presented.

Speaking of being exposed, there was one part of the drill where the brass ensemble slowly gathered into a huge triangle on the fifty yard line, and just as the musical phrase ended with a roar, the whole form turned and went backfield leaving my son John (the point of the triangle) all alone, front and center, playing a sizzling hot solo. I felt so proud that my insides started to bubble.

That afternoon, I met the brass ensemble in a cozy little courtyard, which was the perfect size to comfortably hold a fully integrated circle. The setting was perfect for what I had in mind. We were going to work on creating and capturing the appropriate mood for the closing production, *Since I Fell For You*. I chose an integrated circle because I wanted the bass voice to be omnipresent. After a brief warm-up and tuning, I discussed the tempo, the feel of the tempo, and how they could lightly sway, in a dreamy kind of way. (The tempo I chose for that part of the rehearsal was on the slow slide to emphasize the dreamy aspect of the melodic line).

Once everyone was feeling loose and light, I had the contrabasses lay down their flowing, walking bass line. The contrabasses were spread throughout the circle, evenly intermixed with the rest of the brass ensemble. The resonance in the courtyard was perfect, as was the presence of a light, refreshing breeze rustling the leaves of a few small trees. Once the contrabasses started to groove, I had the soprano soloist layer the melodic line over the bass line. It was about then that the general sway among the performers began to feel and look natural.

We established the dynamic rise and fall of each of the two musical lines. It became immediately apparent to all that there was a strong interaction between the melody and bass. It felt as if the bass voice was providing the motion for the soprano melody to ride upon. As the two voices played together, I could feel the rest of the ensemble getting a little antsy: they wanted to play too! So I layered in the baritones, euphoniums, and altos, who provided a lush, slow-moving chord structure that had the effect of breathing life into the musical phrase.

The excitement was beginning to generate goosebumps. I had the big horns put their instruments down and asked the sopranos and altos to play the full out melody that came after the soprano solo. It began with an extremely strong octave statement that sent shivers up and down the spine. Everyone was hyped! I absolutely loved when that happened. We took the tune from the top, at a slightly faster tempo, and succeeded once again in creating one of those ultra-magical "frozen in time" moments of pure musical madness.

Chapter 39
1988 Competition Season and DCI Fiasco

In the spring of 1988, my lovely wife Edie took me down to the local Honda dealer and bought me a brand spanking new, bright yellow CRX Si with all the trimmings. The car had been nicknamed the pocket rocket, and after driving it home I concurred completely. It was fast, quick, nimble, and cute. And it had a great stereo!

We also moved from our ten-year home (with the huge backyard) in Concord, California, to our beautiful home in Martinez, California, where we have resided happily for the past twenty-two years.

I was forty-six years old in 1988, and I was considering what the future might hold for me. I somehow knew I was coming to a crossroads in the not too distant future, but I had no idea what my options were going to be. I'd been teaching world-class drum and bugle corps for over twenty years and had experienced all the opportunities and successes one could possibly wish for.

But now, the old 'what now' question was buzzing in the back of my mind again. I knew that barring any unforeseen catastrophes, the 1988 Blue Devil brass ensemble was going to be the most musical brass ensemble ever in the history of the drum corps activity, but I also knew that the only things holding me to the Blue Devils drum corps were my two sons John and Tim.

The management and staff of the Blue Devils had been behaving in ways that mocked the reasons that had brought me to the corps in 1978. I no longer felt at ease with the staff. The Blue Devils drum corps was no longer a place for me to work and build my dreams.

But performing with the Blue Devils was something both of my sons had been working toward for nine years, and I was not going to let them down. So I did what I have always done, I put it all on the back burner and provided time over the next few years to do some investigative daydreaming concerning my future creative endeavors.

* * *

The 1988 Blue Devils did not wear spats. As a matter of fact, the uniforms they wore weren't even blue. The director had taken it upon himself to change the image of the six-time world champion Blue Devils. He chose black jackets, grey pants, and grey patent leather shoes. The colorguard wore long, white, flowing gowns with beautifully plumed headdresses. Each of the colorguard ladies danced with a big blue balloon on a string, which they released dramatically into the air at the conclusion of the *Happy Days* production.

The new look for the brass and percussion performers lacked visual impact, the grey slacks and grey shoes were virtually lost against the green turf. But it wasn't enough of a negative to detract from the magnificence of the brass ensemble, or the visual beauty of the colorguard.

Two of the most creative Blue Devil staff members, Shirley Stratton and Stephanie Lynde, had been designing Blue Devil colorguard shows for many years, but their inventiveness and musicality knew no bounds when it came to the '88 show.

The Blue Devil colorguard was beautiful as always. The ladies moved beautifully, with a mature style and grace, through routines that would test the prowess of a gold medal athlete, all the while smiling happily. Shirley and Stephanie also took a hand in choreographing visuals that year for the brass performers in the *Goodbye Yesterday* production. They challenged the performers with fancy footwork and full body dance moves, all of which had to be accomplished while producing some of the finest musical sounds I had ever heard.

The 1988 Blue Devil brass ensemble was so capable when it came to controlling dynamics that they could actually transpose volume levels. They could shift from full out playing mode to mezzo forte playing mode while maintaining all dynamic contrasts and full focused intensity.

There are several very important benefits derived from acquiring this degree of dynamic facility. When volume levels are brought down, performers can hear one another more discretely, which allows for a more unanimous style of musical expression. Performing at lower dynamic levels is also less fatiguing, and helps to encourage clear, easy tone, which promotes strong embouchure development.

But my personal favorite benefit derived from practicing at mezzo forte volume levels is that when the performers are finally permitted to play full out, it's like opening the floodgates of heaven. It's like experiencing, first hand, the thrill of riding the back of a racehorse running flat out. Why, it's like attending the famous finale where the fat lady finally sings.

Seventy motivated brass performers, artfully resonating the spatial molecular environment around one's entire being in a frenzied performance of auditory brilliance, is a treat beyond measure… I love it!

* * *

The 1988 California tour was once again a complete reversal of fortunes. As hard as Santa Clara tried, they could not catch the Blue Devils. The Vanguard had a great show that year, based on Andrew Lloyd Webber's *Phantom of the Opera*. But the Blue Devils consistently scored between a point and a half and three points above them.

By the time the two corps reached Denver, Colorado, Santa Clara had a string of eleven second place showings and the Blue Devils stood undefeated.

That night at the Denver show the Vanguard scored an 86.8 and the Blue Devils scored an 89.0.

At the DCI Midwest championship in Whitewater, Wisconsin, (one week later) the Blue Devils scored a 91.9, the Vanguard a 90.2, and the Madison Scouts an 87.3.

At the DCI East championship in Allentown, (one week later) the Blue Devils scored a 93.7, Star of Indiana a 91.5, the Garfield Cadets a 90.9, and the Cavaliers a 90.8.

Four days later, on August 10th in Bloomington, Indiana, The Blue Devils rocked the drum corps world with a 95.200 over the Cavaliers' 93.3 and Star's 92.4.

At this point in the season, I received word that the buzz going around at critiques (I almost never went to critiques, but I did listen to select judges tapes) was that the Madison Scouts (and the rest of the Midwest) were getting a big push. Along with this, the judges were now telling the Blue Devils that the corps' visual show was not difficult enough, and that the percussion section was exhibiting execution problems.

* * *

DCI world Championship preliminaries were held in Kansas City, Missouri, nine days later on August 19th. The two top performing drum corps going into the prelim competition were the Blue Devils, who had gone through the entire season undefeated, and the Santa Clara Vanguard, who were also undefeated, except for when they competed against the Blue Devils. By analyzing contest scores for the entire season I would say that the Garfield Cadets would have been in the third spot and the Star of Indiana fourth. Past that were the Cavaliers, Phantom Regiment, Madison Scouts, and the Velvet Knights rounding out the top eight corps in the world.

The Blue Devils 1988 DCI preliminary performance was their finest show of the year to date, but they had to leave the competition without knowing their score. As a matter of fact, no scores were announced at the preliminary competition. All of the corps left the show that evening without having been informed of the results.

We heard rumors later on that we had lost prelims by a large margin. And we heard through the grapevine that instead of the top twelve corps going on in reverse order of finish (as they always had in the past) there would be a drawing held to set the order of appearance for the final competition.

What was going on? I for one could not believe that this was happening, and I could only hope that someone would come along to put things right. But sadly, no one was going to ride in on a white horse and save the day. There were no men like Jim Jones or Jerry Seawright left on the DCI board of directors to stand up for what was right.

The Blue Devil director, who had been working single-handedly to convert the classy, yet ruggedly individualistic style of Jerry Seawright's Blue Devils to a kinder, gentler, more compliant manner, went along blissfully with the sham of the DCI director, and somehow managed to draw one of the worst possible positions for the Blue Devils' final appearance.

It was unthinkable! The sky would still be light when the corps went on the field. The chances of winning even so much as a caption award would be practically nil. The traditional interpretation of the judging rules made it virtually impossible for a corps to win from the position of fifth or sixth from the end.

(That's why it had always been so important for the corps to perform its best in the preliminary round; position of appearance meant everything when it came down to the final outcome.)

While on the subject of final outcomes, this is a statement the Director of DCI made shortly prior to the final competition: On any given night, any one of the top eight drum corps in the competition could win the championship.

But the truth of the matter is that on any given night, if you are not in the top three spots going into finals, your chances of winning the championship are lower than if you were to bet the wrong way on a rigged boxing match. And, to anyone who has experienced and studied drum corps' performances over the years, the truth of the matter is that among the top three drum corps in the world there is almost always (nine times out of ten) a clear winner.

The Blue Devils, who had won every contest that year against all comers, and almost always by multiple points, placed second in GE brass, third in GE percussion, sixth in GE visual, fifth in percussion performance, fourth in visual performance, and believe it or not, first in brass. That made eight high brass awards in the ten years I had been with the corps.

The corps that won the 1988 DCI championship possessed several very important qualifications that the Blue Devils did not. First and foremost, they were not from California. Second, they did hail from the good ole Midwest. Third, they had an obvious theme to their show (Spanish music), and fourth, they were celebrating their fiftieth anniversary.

In addition to these key attributes, throughout the last two and a half weeks of the competitive season, their scores miraculously ascended a whopping ten points, which was by far the largest score increase during that time period in all of drum corps history. Truly a miracle when compared to the Blue Devils' mere four and a half point increase, or the Vanguard's six and a half point increase, or the Star of Indiana's four and a half point increase, or the Velvet Knights four and a half points increase.

Totally amazing!

The corps who won the 1988 DCI championship has never again won a DCI World title, nor have they ever again placed in the top three spots at finals.

The idea of holding a drawing to determine the order of appearance at the final competition has never been used again at the DCI World Championships. Since the 1988 fiasco, drum corps have again had to earn their place in the final round of competition by virtue of the quality of their performance in the semi-final round of competition.

Chapter 40
1989 Resignation

In September of 1988 I was asked to develop a music program for the new Golden View Elementary School. This was in addition to my existing program with Bollinger Canyon. I also decided to take on a series of winter clinics with two Canadian drum corps: Allegiance Elite in Calgary, Alberta, and the Ventures in Toronto. As I said before, there was no doubt in my mind that my work with the Blue Devils was coming to an end.

Somehow I knew that the 1988 brass ensemble would be my final great achievement in drum corps. This became especially clear when I was informed of the director's musical choices for the '89 season. The 1989 Blue Devil musical repertoire was as innovative as the all black uniform the director was having the corps wear that year.

For the life of me, I could not understand the intelligence or motivation behind the A corps director's decision to change the image of the most spectacular drum corps in the world. Why would a person do that? The only answer that comes to mind is ego: one huge, monumental ego.

But as for me, the straw that broke the camel's back was perpetrated against a soprano player in the corps. His name was Dan. It was tryout night for the closing set of solos in the second production. Dan was auditioning for the main solo, and my son Tim was auditioning for the second solo.

Dan made the solo his own and aimed his musical direction toward a sustained double high C, then nimbly made his way back down into normal range.

No doubt, the performance was a complete blowaway, and Dan and Tim were awarded the solo duet on the spot by the brass caption head. (This would never have happened in the past without the two of us discussing the solo and the choice of soloists).

My problem with allowing the solo to stand as played was the amount of pressure that would be placed on the soloist. A double high C in a lyrical solo is unusual at best. Few, if any, of the other performers in the corps could have played this particular solo even once. And aside from the technical difficulty, the solo was completely exposed; it was like walking a wiggly tight rope, over a fire pit, jam-packed with fireproof, man-eating sharks.

As the solo ascended in pitch to the high point of the musical phrase everything stopped, save for a muted, backfield chord. All responsibility for the success of the show was placed squarely on Dan's shoulders. The whole corps froze in place. He was totally alone. Common sense would state, and the law of averages would dictate, that there would be performances when he would miss the note (blow the solo). And when he did, the whole drum corps would be left waiting for him to somehow pick up the thread and lead them back in.

I pleaded with those in charge not to put that young man in a position of such ultimate pressure, but my pleadings fell on deaf ears. The brass caption head had made his mind up.

From that point on I could no longer muster the slightest amount of respect for either the brass caption head or the corps director, and resolved in the future to have no more to do with either one of them.

* * *

I did my best that year to remain positive and upbeat, but the fact was that I felt as though I were beating my head against a stone wall. The staff was in complete disarray. At one point in the season a staff meeting was called. It was to be held at Rod's Pizza. I think everyone figured out what the meeting was about when they noticed that the A corps director had not been invited.

We had the whole place to ourselves. When orders were taken and the food was served, the discussion began. One faction of the staff was completely dissatisfied with the direction the corps was taking. These were mostly people who had marched with the Blue Devils back in the '70s, and who remembered how things had been when Jerry Seawright was director. On the other side of the discussion were the higher paid caption heads who knew all too well which side their bread was buttered on, and so, wanted things to remain status quo. As for myself, I didn't say much because I knew nothing decisive would come from the meeting. The staff was so divided by then that there was no way they could come together to formulate an intelligent plan of action; when people are constantly put in a position of doing only what they are told, they tend to lose their individual sense of power and initiative. The meeting ended dismally, leaving everyone totally frustrated.

The next day I submitted my letter of resignation to the Blue Devil board of directors, effective midnight, the evening of finals.

Chapter 41
1989 The Season

1989 turned out to be a very busy year for me, what with teaching the Blue Devils, conducting two full time elementary school programs (four days a week), and taking too many quick trips to Canada. When late spring finally rolled around, between rehearsals, getting ready for performances, and conducting performances with the elementary bands, the Blue Devils and the Canadian corps, I was beat: mentally, physically, and emotionally. I was hoping the summer drum corps season would serve as a vacation by comparison. But a summer vacation it was not to be.

During the 1989 season I experienced first hand what high stress levels can do to people. It wasn't a pretty sight. For the first time ever, my son John experienced lip problems, which included swelling and discoloration. Dan, the double C soloist was experiencing conflicts in his personal life (which was very unusual, because Dan had been a well mannered, easy going young man since joining the corps in 1986), and he was having performance problems with the double C in a few of the victory concerts.

Along with all of this, a few disgruntled instructors had taken to chanting, "we're hurtin' ... for certain ..." throughout the tour. There was little in the way of cross caption, or even intracaption camaraderie. Personal communication was at a standstill. I was discovering just how stressful it could be, heading down the road on a thirty-day tour with everyone knowing all too well that the corps' show would never get off the ground.

The brass ensemble played extremely well that season, but since the musical selections were not as inspired as one might hope (that is to

say that the show did not take the listener from here to there), the performers' attitudes suffered. The opening production was a remix of the
1981 opener, *Ya Gotta Try*, and the closing production was a remix of
the 1981 closer, *Johnny One Note*. Sandwiched between these two ret-
rofitted pillars from the past was a duet of musically forgettable tunes,
the titles of which escape me. I honestly thought the caption head was
pulling my leg when he played the recordings for the first time, but I
was most emphatically assured, right then and there, that the musical
selections were not a joke.

* * *

It was all the Blue Devils could do to eke out a small victory over
the Star of Indiana on first tour. Of the thirty shows that season, the Blue
Devils won five, tied for first place in two, and placed second, third,
and fourth in the rest. I found it extremely difficult to become enthused
about working a show that held no musical interest for me. It was like
polishing an old rock: you can buff it up clean and bright, but when all
is said and done it's still just a rock.

In order to create something special, there must first be something
special to work with. I had a great brass ensemble, but all we had to play
were exercises; performing the 1989 show was an exercise in frustration. No matter how well the hornline played, it wasn't going to sell. It
was missing three magical ingredients: traditional Blue Devil swagger,
musical continuity, and crisp ensemble performance.

Without the musical swagger of Blue Devil tradition there was no
sense of history, no time-honored strength of image. Without musical
continuity, the qualities of drama and intrigue were virtually neutral-
ized. And without unanimous musical intention there was little chance
for emotional impact.

I think for the first time in my life I was truly stressing.

It was no fun!

* * *

In 1989, the Santa Clara Vanguard had reprised their show from the previous year, drawing on music from the Broadway hit, *Phantom of the Opera*. Their '89 competitive season was identical to the Blue Devils' '86 competitive season: undefeated except for one show, which happened to be the Blue Devils' home show in Concord... and it was only fitting that it was the Blue Devils who handed them their singular defeat of the year.

* * *

The Blue Devils' final performance for 1989 was a direct reflection of the four days leading up it. We had been housed at a school with no stadium facilities, no bleachers, and no vantage point from which to balance and adjust the show. The only rehearsal field the corps had to work with reminded me of the rodeo grounds in Casper, Wyoming, only drier. It was uneven, and came complete with potholes, weeds, and an uphill slant. The whole situation was tragically reminiscent of how poorly both the tour and the entire season had gone.

The corps entered the field on finals night as the Blue Devils, but looked more like the Black and White Knights. Edie and I were seated in the fourth row of the lower deck, at about the thirty-five yard line, directly behind my old friend Pepe Nataro from the New York Skyliners. Pepe was the loudest, funniest human being I had ever known.

Pepe asked me, "Jacky! Why the hell aint they wearing blue?" loud enough for the whole stands to hear him. I shrugged my shoulders as though to say, "don't ask me." Pepe rolled his eyes, pantomimed a Brooklyn wise guy expression with his whole body, slapped me on the knee and turned back to watch the show.

(Earlier that day, the corps had been bused to the housing site of the Velvet Knights, who were staying at a great facility, complete with stadium. The VK had been kind enough to allow the corps to rehearse at their site for a period of time that morning. Halfway through the rehearsal run-through the water sprinklers came on and drenched everyone on the field. The corps was totally frustrated and knew that their next run-through would be their last).

Like a true thoroughbred, the Blue Devils exploded out of the gate with pent-up emotions, pent-up frustrations, and a burning desire to leave it all out on the field. Tempo was brisk, enthusiasm was up, the sound was clear and bright.

Whenever the corps was on the field, I felt as though huge amounts of energy flowed from my heart out to the performers. This was especially true with soloists. I lived and breathed every note with them. I was completely alive within the sound of their performance as it happened; it was all good positive energy.

The corps sailed through to the solo section of *Ya Gotta Try*. First up was Rich Zeller, a fine performer and soloist with the Blue Devils since 1987. Rich and my son John shared the solo work in the opening production and they were both on fire that evening. They were totally captivating!

At the completion of the opening production I would have said that the performers were at the top of their game. They were hot, and they were rocking the house.

The drum major gave the command to begin the second production. The contrabasses laid out their introductory bass line, after which John and Rich performed the ballad duet to a tee, expertly handing it off to the full ensemble who proceeded to paint the audience with a full throated musical sound that danced and sparkled with brilliance.

It was time for Dan, three year Blue Devil veteran, and my young son Tim to put the final touches on a wonderful performance of the second production.

(The amount of stress placed on Dan throughout the last two weeks of the tour had prompted his parents to call members of the Blue Devil board of directors demanding that their son be sent home immediately, but Dan decided to stay. It was not a good scene, and the consequences of his decision to stay would be far reaching for Dan, for his family, and for the Blue Devils).

The time had come for the deal breaker, the all-important note, the double high C.

Tim played his lead-in phrase exquisitely, foreshadowing Dan's double C with a double A of his own. Dan sounded his pick up notes and surged into the upper register of the instrument, aiming for the double high C. The note was there, for the briefest of moments, then disappeared in a rush of air… For a seeming eternity nothing happened… No one moved… Forty thousand fans sat in stunned silence. I felt as though the bottom had fallen out of my heart. The whole corps seemed to sag, as did the sustained chord in the low brass. Dan tried again but nothing came out. (Tim says he will never forget Dan's agonizing groan of "aw crap Tim" as he tried again and again to regain the musical thread to lead the corps back in). Dan eventually tumbled down through a jumble of notes, and ended on the right pitch so that Tim, and the whole corps, could finally resume.

I was devastated! I was devastated for Dan, for Tim, for John, for every kid out on that field. My mind was screaming inside of my head that this should never have happened. I will never understand how those kids pulled it all back together after that, but they did. They made me proud.

The show concluded with Dan, John, Rich, and Tim screaming away (playing high and loud) on the sideline as though nothing untoward had happened… But something had happened. And it was one of those deep, dark, terrible somethings that a person never ever forgets.

Part Three

Transitions

Chapter 42
1990 Crossmen and Velvet Knights

The Santa Clara Vanguard went on to win the 1989 DCI World title, after having placed second in '85, '86, '87, and '88. And the corps who had miraculously won the DCI World title the past year, in 1988, namely the Madison Scouts, placed seventh.

The Blue Devils placed fourth overall with a 95.9 to Santa Clara's winning score of 98.8. It would not be until 1994 that the Blue Devils would find their way out of fourth and fifth place to win their seventh DCI World title, eight years after winning their last title in 1986.

* * *

The thought had occurred to me that my future with drum corps was winding down. But at forty-seven years of age, I was at the top of my game. I was still vital!

I wasn't winding down!

I found it hard to envision a future without drum corps; the creative substitute had not yet effervesced in my mind. I had no inklings, no glimmers, no notions, no sparks. All I had was that old nagging mantra pulsing through the corridors of my brain: What now? What's next? Am I done yet?

One thing was for sure, I wasn't done yet. John was eighteen and Tim was fifteen. For sure I wasn't done yet. John was a freshman at the local junior college, starring in his role as featured soloist with the jazz band, and Tim was busy being a sophomore in high school. Neither of the boys wished to go back to the Blue Devils.

Edie had finished all of the course work and licensing tests necessary to become a loan officer for Bank of America, and I was still working my two elementary music programs and doing weekend trips to Canada. Things were just fine as far as I was concerned. But over the next five years, I would work with five more drum corps, Tim would march and solo with four drum corps, and John would write three complete drum corps shows.

* * *

In early October of 1989 I received a call from Bobby Hoffman, famed originator of the Bayonne Bridgemen, and top show designer for many successful drum and bugle corps. Bobby was designing a show for the Velvet Knights in southern California and asked if I would like to take over the brass program. A few days later I received a call from Carl Ruocco, an old friend from Skyliner days, asking if I would like to take over the brass program for the Crossmen drum and bugle corps out of South Jersey. The Lord does work in mysterious ways. How could I refuse? I would be working with friends! Friends from the old days! How cool was that? I accepted both offers.

It was a scheduling nightmare, though. Each of the corps had to set their rehearsal schedule around my schedule. It worked out that I had camp weekends three out of four weekends a month, which meant flying out on a Friday morning and arriving home by Sunday evening. By early Monday morning I was back to teaching elementary school at Bollinger Canyon. It was a good thing I truly loved to teach…

I did have the chance to build my frequent flyer miles up, though. Of course, it meant flying on crowded airplanes, running frantically through busy airports, making connections, missing connections, and being bumped by stewardesses' hips and their serving carts (I always chose to sit in the aisle seat).

Then there was always the dilemma of lugging luggage, losing luggage, and flying on those scary little commuter flights. It was all great fun, though. I had the opportunity to be with good friends and to work with some very talented young instructors and arrangers.

Mike Collins, featured soprano soloist for the Blue Devils in 1986, headed up the in-town brass staff for the VK. Mike knew my program and understood how I went about things almost as well as I did. We got along famously.

The east coast arranger that Bobby Hoffman had brought on board to write the musical book for the VK didn't come through, so Bobby went out and found a bright new arranger from the Deep South. Brad Pearson was his name. Brad had never written for drum corps, only for bands, but once he got his feet wet, his arrangements began to blaze with color and musical inventiveness. Brad was fun to work with and great to hang out with.

But before Brad could come on line with the VK, I asked my son John to write an arrangement for me so I would have something to teach the brass ensemble at our first camp. John came up with a cool rendition of *Under the Boardwalk* as performed by the Drifters. It was John's first arrangement. It was one of those last minute situations, so he had to do it in less than two days. The VK brass ensemble loved it. So did my son Tim.

Tim had asked to go along with me that weekend to check out the corps. He sat in with the hornline on Friday night and had a ball. He was only 15 years of age at the time, but because he had been a featured soloist with the Blue Devils, he was treated like a drum corps icon at the VK rehearsal. Chuck Betz, a great soloist and a super guy, became Tim's best buddy that night.

* * *

With the Crossmen, I was teamed up with Carl Ruocco, director, and Dennis Delucia, program coordinator. Carl (a good friend from Skyliner days) was a percussionist turned director, and Dennis (from Muchachos, Bridgemen, and Star of Indiana fame) was a percussionist extraordinaire turned program coordinator. Along with these two drum corps legends, I had the opportunity to work with Mark Thurston and his wonderful staff of percussion instructors. They were very young, very talented, and totally committed to producing a percussion section that was both precise and musical. Mark's score writing as well as his approach to teaching reminded me a great deal of Fred Sanford's work with Santa Clara back in the late '60s. Mark was very intense, but easy-going, with a laid back manner.

* * *

In January of 1990, my son John traveled to Toronto to take over my work with the Ventures all-girl drum and bugle corps. At nineteen years of age, John had decided that his marching days were over, and that he would like to try his hand at teaching. His years in the Blue Devils had afforded him many opportunities to experience the art of performance at the highest possible levels. His musicianship, his temperament, and his supreme sense of self-confidence made John a natural when it came to instructing and motivating young people.

John told me after his first trip to Toronto that a few of the girls in the Ventures wanted to hear him play his Blue Devil solos "live" for them.

That is like oh, so, cool!

Chapter 43
1990 The Season

Experiencing the drum corps activity from so many varied points of view gave me a better understanding of what actually separated the top three or four corps from the rest of the pack. Certainly talent had something to do with it: the talent level of the staff, the talent level of the performers. But what I found to be the number one factor in making the final ascent to the top three was the attitude of the staff, management, and performers toward rehearsal time.

Rehearsal time was the life-blood of the early Casper Troopers. Beginning each year the rehearsal emphasis was placed strictly on the basics: step size, posture, and work ethic, with an acute awareness of space, distance, alignment, and the sound of Mr. Jones' voice. The Troopers were well drilled in the fundamental commands of attention, left turn, right turn, forward march, about face, etc. etc.

Observation, correction, and repetition were the tools used to mold the corps into a precision unit.

As the year progressed, the emphasis switched from drilling on basics to learning and practicing the show's many maneuvers until the complex movements became second nature. If the basics were embedded strongly enough in the performers' psyche, then everything would eventually fall into place.

For Jim Jones and the Troopers, rehearsal time was sacred, especially while on tour. If a bus broke down the corps would be found rehearsing in the local supermarket parking lot, or at a rest stop, or on the side of the road. Nothing got in the way of the corps' constant improvement. After competitive show critiques, Mr. Jones would hold an hour-long critique with the whole corps to go over every tic on the sheets: observation, correction, repetition.

The same was true of the Santa Clara Vanguard. Fred Sanford and Pete Emmons had learned their lessons well from Mr. Jones. The Vanguard was famous for rehearsing right up until it was time to suit up and go out onto the field to perform.

It all came down to a firm commitment and complete dedication to getting it right. The staff ignited the flame and the corps burned with it. Every performer became invested in the idea of improving their part in the show. The individuals in the corps began to feel they could improve daily, more than they had ever dreamed possible. Over the season every performer learned to do the impossible, or at least what they had thought was impossible.

* * *

In my mind, the aim of any rehearsal is to lay the proper groundwork, to create the perfect situation, making it possible for performers to intuitively experience that which they might never have imagined. Well-designed, properly directed experiences guide performers toward an innate understanding of both the art and process of performance. Their mindsets become appropriate to the task at hand; they learn to progress through the experiential tool of achievement.

* * *

The problem I faced in the winter and spring of 1990 was a drastic cut in available hours of rehearsal time. Rehearsal time went from thirty or forty hours per month with the Blue Devils to nine hours per month with each of the three corps. I had to drastically change the way I worked. And I had to rein in my expectations of what would be possible to achieve. It became more and more obvious to me that the brightest stars in the universe of brass performance were eluding my grasp.

* * *

The 1990 DCI World Championships were held at Rich Stadium in Buffalo, New York. Edie and I had decided early on to put a little honeymoon into our trip out east. First of all, we would get to see our boys for championship week, and we would have the opportunity to take a little moonlight drive to Niagara Falls for some well-deserved rest and recreation.

We had great seats at finals: second row, second tier, forty-yard line, starting line side. We didn't get to our seats until just before the Crossmen entered the field. Edie had decided to accompany me as I prepared the Velvet Knights and the Crossmen brass ensembles for competition that evening. During the warm ups, we were interviewed by Dennis Delucia for the DCI network TV show. Normally I shied away from interviews, but with Dennis it was okay.

The finals show that night was truly a great final presentation. All of the corps sparkled under the bright lights of Rich stadium. I was very pleased with both the Velvet Knights and Crossmen presentations. Both brass ensembles played very well. Their performances were musical, clear, and intense.

Edie and I enjoyed seeing the top corps establish their individual personalities right before our eyes. Each of them had always conveyed an intense personal image to me. Each corps had a character, a look, a way of moving, or a style of music that set them apart. They each demonstrated qualities and traits, traditions and rituals that anchored them to the activity of drum and bugle corps.

The 1990 finals presentation was no different. Each corps in turn demonstrated their particular web of intrigue, their own personal individualized recipe for entertainment. It was truly magical. But the corps that captured my interest most, the corps that held me in the palm of their hand, was the Cadets of Bergen County. I had seen them perform earlier in the season and thought at the time they had a great show but that it was doubtful they would ever be able to pull it off.

It was an extremely difficult show from every aspect. It was crammed full of musical emotions, which were beautifully interpreted through visual forms and transitions. The percussion program was a complete show in itself!

The final competitive performance of the 1990 Cadets of Bergen County was one of those great drum corps performances that epitomize what the drum corps activity is all about: hard work, dedication, innovation, and miles of heart.

The Crossmen improved from a twelfth place finish in 1989 to seventh place in 1990, and the VK improved from eleventh place to tenth place. The Allegiance Elite from Calgary, Canada had moved up from 14th place in A class competition in 1988 to 9th place in 1990, and the Ventures from Toronto won the class A championship in 1990, just as they had in 1989.

Chapter 44
Tim and the Crossmen

My son John was now living and teaching in Toronto. He was also falling in love with one of the lead alto players of the Ventures all girl drum and bugle corps.

My son Tim had experienced a great year with the Velvet Knights. He made a few wonderful friendships, turned sweet sixteen, and played his heart out on the field of competition. What more could a guy ask?

* * *

The supreme highlight of the 1991 drum corps season was seeing my sixteen year old son Tim play the role of featured soloist for the Crossmen's new show. Tim wanted to travel back east with me because he longed for the touch and feel of snow. He had been born in New Jersey, but spent his second, third, and fourth years in Casper, Wyoming, where it would get very cold, but very dry; the snow flakes felt like soft wisps of cotton as they fell. I said to Tim, "along with east coast snow comes bone chilling cold," to which he responded, "bring it on."

We arrived in Philadelphia in the late afternoon. The sun was disappearing into the western sky. Tim and I retrieved our bags and waited for our ride. There was an accumulation of snow lying just outside the doors but it didn't look too fresh or clean, so Tim didn't mind waiting inside.

Carl Ruocco pulled up on the other side of the roadway and waved, gesturing for us to come ahead. We pushed though the doors and had advanced only about fifteen feet when I heard a loud grunt from Tim. I turned to see what was up. Tim looked as though he had been hit in the gut with a baseball bat. He was pulling his jacket over his chest, his teeth were chattering. He turned to me, shaking, and said in a quivery voice, "it's really cold."

So much for "bring it on."

Dennis Delucia had come up with a wonderful new musical show for 1991 using the rhythmic melodies of Pat Metheny. *Minuano, Dream of the Return, Last Train,* and *Third Wind* formed a cohesive musical package that challenged and showcased both the brass and percussion sections.

The corps had a fantastic first camp with a large crop of talented new performers. The difficulty was that the corps had no instruments for them to play. Of the instruments left over from the 1990 season, only about eighty percent were usable. There were eighty-five brass players and only forty-five instruments. Sorry to say that only a handful of the new recruits who had come to the first camp ended up coming back for the second camp.

I had to give Tim my personal three-valve King soprano so he could perform with the corps. The management eventually found a way to purchase a much-needed set of three-valve alto instruments from Zig Kanstul, and along with the order came a donation from Zig of two three-valve soprano bugles.

Unlike the Blue Devils, who had created a million dollar bingo enterprise over the years, the Crossmen had no predictable income; the money just wasn't there, but the hard work, dedication, and determination were. These were east coast kids and they reminded me of the Muchachos. They were bright, aware, and ready to learn. And everybody was a wise guy.

I'll never forget the time I cut the hornline during a brass rehearsal for something I was hearing from the lead baritone section. Signaling for the hornline to bring their instruments down I found myself looking in the direction of one performer in particular. As I stepped toward the young man who had now fixed his gaze on me, I heard him say in a loud, clear, musical voice, "Don't look at me" and in unison the whole hornline delivered the line, "I didn't do it."

There was one very special event for me in the '91 Crossmen show.

My son Tim was left standing all alone, front and center on the fifty. Surrounding Tim were a dozen beautiful colorguard girls with large blue and green shawls, swirling round and round. The music and drill were approaching a major climax. At the zenith of the phrase the colorguard spun open like a flower, exposing Tim as he wailed away on the plaintive melody of *Dream of the Return*. It was one of those breath-grabbing, heart-pounding moments that every proud Papa lives for. Tim was as captivating a soloist as I had ever had the pleasure of mentoring.

He's a kid he's a man he's an angel he's a joy
He's the best in the world he's my Timmy he's my boy
And if you ever saw him you surely would agree
That a handsomer young man you never did see
So big and so tall, with eyes dark and bright
And a smile to chase your cares out of sight...
I cherish the times he made me so proud
Raised his horn on high and played for the crowd
And how down through the years he conquered his fears
Played high and sweet bringing the crowd to their feet
But if truth be told, what's most special about Tim
Is the warm happy feeling that comes from just being with him

Chapter 45
1991 Bob Adair and Liberty Bell Cadets

It was the DCI Eastern Classic Championship competition held at J. Birney Crum Stadium in Allentown, Pennsylvania, 1991. J. Birney Crum Stadium was the scene of the Blue Devils' only defeat during the 1980 season: Allentown! The eastern stronghold.

I was there with the Crossmen, who were doing very well by that point in the year. They had started the season poorly but worked very hard to improve their performance capabilities. The weather in the stadium was hot and humid as always on prelims day in Allentown. I was standing under a big shade tree adjacent to where the corps enter and leave the competition field. The huge old tree had long been a gathering place for instructors and drum corps enthusiasts alike to cool down from the intense heat of prelims. I often thought that if I stood there long enough I would eventually meet everybody who was anybody in drum corps.

While cooling off in the shade, I was approached by my good friend Tommy Martin. Tommy introduced me to a gentleman standing next to him. His name was Bobby Adair. I was dumbfounded. Bob Adair was a living legend in east coast drum corps. He had been the arranger and instructor for the Liberty Bell Cadets through the '50s, and the arranger, instructor, and soloist for the Reilly Raiders, a senior drum corps from Philadelphia, during the late '50s.

Liberty Bell was my absolute favorite drum corps in the whole world when I was growing up. There was something about their sound that was like no other. It sparkled with the brilliant sound of high sopranos.

Not only did the soprano line play the melodies, they played the counter line obbligato parts too.

Liberty Bell's brass ensemble played notes that no other drum corps played. That was because they cheated. They pulled their tuning slides out to play the chromatic notes of the scale. Pulling tuning slides was illegal in VFW competition. Corps had to have tape wrapped around the tuning slide ferrules to prevent the slides from being pulled out. But Liberty Bell figured a way around the rule with a razor blade, or so the story goes, and played illegal notes to their hearts content. Imagine that, illegal notes in music. You could actually hear the slides being snapped back in place after being pulled for a chromatic note. The sharp click of the slides became part of the Liberty Bell experience.

In those days, junior corps hornlines usually numbered between twenty and thirty members. The instruments that Liberty Bell used were soprano bugles and small bell baritone bugles. They had no alto or bass instruments. The sopranos played the melody, while harmonic rhythms were layered in with lower soprano and baritone voices. Counter lines were played by obbligato sopranos with low octave support.

Liberty Bell's lead soprano lines were blessed with many very fine, strong, musical performers. In contrast to today's twelve minute drum corps show, shows back then ran as long as fifteen minutes. The brass ensemble played most of those fifteen minutes, and in Liberty Bell's case the lead soprano line played almost all the time. The acoustic aura produced by the Liberty Bell Cadets was music to my ears, and their brass instructor, Bob Adair, was my muse and inspiration.

I had never had the good fortune to meet Mr. Adair before that day in Allentown, but through his arrangements, and the wonderful performers he produced, he single handedly generated a deep desire, need, and ambition in me to assist in bringing about what I have come to think of as the audio image of silver rain: high screaming sopranos.

But it wasn't until just recently that I discovered that it was Bob Adair who played the *Stardust* solo in 1958 with the Reilly Raiders. No one had ever heard anything like it before. Bob Adair absolutely captivated the audience with the beauty of his tone and the professional musical portrayal he brought to the dreamy melodic line of *Stardust*. My understanding of how Liberty Bell had acquired such a strong, musical lead line was finally complete. When normally talented young people are exposed to the musical talents of a man like Bob Adair great things can happen, for we are all essentially very talented mimics.

To listen to Bob Adair's solo from 1958 go to:
  http://osmondpostcadets.com/Life%20after%20Osmond.html.
  Scroll down to where it says, "click for Bob's solo."

If you would like to do a little drum corps reminiscing, you can go to:
  http://osmondpostcadets.com/OurCompetitors.html
  Click "competitors," then simply scroll down the list of corps, pick one and click one. My favorites are the Audubon Bon Bons, Blessed Sacrament, Liberty Bell, Holy Name Cadets (Garfield Cadets) and St. Vincents Cadets.

You will hear drum corps recordings from the forties and fifties, and you will see plenty of drum corps snapshots from the long ago past. I find it truly amazing how much one can learn about drum corps history by doing a little in-depth research on the Internet. Much of my specific research on corps history was done at:
  http://www.corpsreps.com/scores.cfm?view=scoremajor

Now back to the Allentown classic...
The Cavaliers won the preliminary competition with the Cadets placing second, the Crossmen third, and here comes the thrill of the afternoon, the Blue Devils fourth. Did you ever have the feeling that you were the cat who just swallowed the bird and that there were feathers spewing out your nose and mouth? To say the least, I was overjoyed. That evening the Crossmen had their best show of the year to date and managed to tie the Blue Devils for second place. The Cavaliers won the show and the Cadets placed fourth.
During the 1991 DCI World Championships held in Dallas, Texas, I

was inducted into the DCI Hall of Fame along with my best drum corps buddies Fred Sanford, George Zingalli, Truman Crawford, and Dennis Delucia. It was a huge honor to be so recognized by the drum corps fraternity. And as if that were not enough, Gail Royer, director of the Santa Clara Vanguard, asked if I would consider taking on the Vanguard brass program for the corps' twenty-fifth anniversary year in 1992. All of that plus the fact that Tim had enjoyed a fantastic solo performance with the Crossmen at finals made it truly a night to remember.

Chapter 46
1992 Santa Clara Vanguard

News Flash!

August 13th 2010. Last night, the Blue Devils once again sailed into the DCI World Championships undefeated, and surged ahead in the competition by winning quarterfinals with a score of 97.900 to the second place Cavaliers score of 96.550

More to come later!

* * *

1992 was a return to the long ago past for me, and a dedication to the future for my family. Edie had agreed one hundred percent with my decision to accept Gail Royer's invitation to oversee the Vanguard brass program for their twenty-fifth anniversary year.

During my very first meeting with Mr. Royer it became evident that he wanted to clean house, and that I should choose a completely new brass staff. So since we were in California, I made my choice from local talent with whom I was familiar, which meant ex Blue Devils. My first choice was Jim McFarland. Jim was soloist for the Blue Devils in 1978, and had worked with the Blue Devil B Corps brass program as well as the A corps contrabass line at various times during the '80s. He had also taken over my instructional responsibilities with the Montreal based Chatelaines Drum and Bugle Corps in 1981.

I asked my son John if he would be interested in working with the Vanguard. The look on his face was that of a kid at Christmas as he bobbed his head up and down with glee. Upon finding out that John was going to teach, my son Tim told us that he had been wanting to march the '92 season with the Vanguard all summer long. Edie wanted to be part of the excitement too and promised moral support and surprise cookie packages during the summer tour.

* * *

News Flash!

The Blue Devils have just won the 2010 DCI World Championship. They have won two straight and have now gone two full years without losing a single competition. The Blue Devil B Corps has just won, for the second year in a row, the DCI Open Class Championship. The B corps has lost only one competition in the past two years.

* * *

So there we were, John, Jim, Tim, and myself, the four of us Blue Devils through and through, walking into the first Santa Clara Vanguard brass rehearsal of the 1992 season. As far as we were concerned it was business as usual: let's get it on. But there was a decided chill in the air from the Vanguard vets. As far as they were concerned we were the enemy; we were the blue guys and they were the red guys.

The first of our group to crack through the emotional ice barrier was my son Tim. All Tim had to do was pick up his horn and play. Tim had the ability to make a piece of music sound exciting and alive. When Tim played his horn, people wanted to listen.

John settled into his particular situation as the alto tech very well. His performance reputation among Northern California corps was almost legendary, and in truth, he was still young enough to march. 1992 would have been his age out year. So John was able to slip in under the vets' radar sweep.

While teaching the Vanguard brass ensemble in 1992 I experienced, for the first time in my life, the feeling of being shunned, dismissed, brushed aside, and there was no way for me to change the mindset of the Vanguard vets. I don't know if you have ever experienced the particular situation of which I speak, but I'm sure you can imagine the sense of absolute frustration born of knowing the unlimited opportunities available if all those concerned took a positive attitude toward the task at hand and got to work.

This problem of misguided loyalties was a huge stumbling block, which I had never even considered as a problematic possibility. There is always a brief period of doubt, uncertainty, and reservation when working with a new group of performers, but nothing that lasts beyond the first few rehearsals. This was different. The defiant attitude of the older vets festered on throughout most of the season.

But I am very happy to say that it did not get in the way of me doing my job, or of enjoying the absolute delight of again working with my sons, John and Tim, or of having the opportunity once again to work with my good buddy Jim McFarland. Opportunities such as these are precious and rare.

The Blue Devilish influence on the Santa Clara Vanguard didn't stop with the four of us. Scott Johnson, the lead Blue Devil snare drummer from 1979, was now heading up the Vanguard percussion program. Scott had been on staff with the Blue Devils throughout the 1980s, resigning his position shortly after finals in 1989.

In some ways it felt like old home week, but in other ways we were forging ahead through uncharted territory. It turned out that in Santa Clara, everything is a tradition, and neither Jim nor I had the slightest idea what ritualistic practice was coming next. All of a sudden another tradition would be upon us and we would have to bob and weave to keep up with the program. Three days before a full corps performance in early spring we were informed that the brass ensemble had to be prepared to play the finale from Phantom of the Opera. I had no idea where to even look for the arrangement. I asked Gail if he had a score, and with a wave of his hand he said, "Oh, they know it." "I'm glad of that" I said, "but I don't know it." He dug around in his files and pulled out a score with parts and copies.

When Gail and I first spoke back in early November, Gail had told me that he was going to have Jim Prime write the musical book for the '92 show. About a month later I was handed a sketch of the opener: *Tradition* from Fiddler on the Roof. It was not arranged by Jim Prime, it was arranged by Gail Royer. It was a hand scribbled rough draft that would take hours of work to render usable. Things weren't supposed to end up that way, but there I was once again, inputting and arranging little notes and rests on my Mac... Why me?

So that was how the year went. Every week was another surprise. In May, John's fiancé Jackie came to California for a visit and decided to stay because she too wanted to play in the Vanguard. Jackie took the last alto spot and the hornline was set.

We won the first show of the year besting the Blue Devils by one point four. It was a sweet victory indeed. But at the next full corps rehearsal I discovered that the whole opening drill had been changed... completely. A very effective minute and a half visual production had been tossed out in favor of a rehearsal nightmare: an old time, updated, starting line, company front extravaganza.

Teaching world-class drum corps was hard enough when things went well, but this was insane. Whole tunes were yanked out of the show in mid season and replaced by completely new productions. Colorguard uniforms and equipment were changed, changed, and changed again. Paranoia, indecision, and change for the sake of change, had become the order of the day.

But all in all, as Frank Sinatra sang so hauntingly, *"It Was a Very Good Year."* Tim absolutely enjoyed the process of becoming a Vanguard performer. He had never been a fan of long, hot marching rehearsals but with the marching staff drilling the disciplined Vanguard work ethic into him he became as invested in the marching program as he had always been in the brass program. As a matter of fact, Tim had become so into being a model Vanguard performer that he actually went out and got a hair cut! No more shoulder length curls... No more ponytail... The Santa Clara Vanguard program had an enormous effect on my almost eighteen-year old son Tim.

On August eighth, 1992, the Santa Clara Vanguard were competing at the DCI Mid America Championship in Bloomington, Indiana. It was one week before the world finals.

I had just finished with the show warm up when I saw my son Tim walking toward me with a worried look on his face. I asked Tim how his warm up had gone and he said, "Dad... I can't play a note." Immediately my heart sank down to my feet. I said, "Is there something wrong with your horn?" as I took his instrument to inspect it. "No, it's not the horn Dad, it's me, there's something wrong with me." I thought my heart would explode out of my sandals.

(Tim had three show stopping solos. He began the show all alone with the first four bars of the *Fiddler* melody for which one admiring judge had dubbed Tim a hero. The end of *Sabbath Prayer* was all Tim, and he ended it with the sweetest double high A you ever heard. Tim also introduced the *"Bottle Dance"* with his wonderful interpretation of the clarinet solo from the original recording. For his over the top theatrical effort, visual designer Myron Rosander nicknamed Tim "the milkman.")

What was I gonna do? What was I gonna say? My number two son was depending on me to get him out of this predicament. I said to him, "Tim, you are the finest horn player I have ever known, and I am sure that what you experienced during the warm up was nothing more than a nervous flutter, a flitter of self doubt that we all experience from time to time. I am confident that you will make me proud and bring them roaring to their feet tonight." I then reached into my pocket and took out a packet of Tic Tacs and handed one to Tim. I said, "hold on to this until you hit the field, then pop it in your mouth and push it down between your cheek and your gums. You're gonna be fine." The corps lined up and off they went.

Now, from what I remember, the stadium was a huge, open bowl. I chose to sit about three quarters of the way up the stands in the end zone. I wanted to be all alone. The crowd was concentrated between the twenty-yard lines. I couldn't believe that I was so nervous. I felt as though my world was about to crumble right before my eyes. I sat and waited, and prayed. The corps came out onto the field. Tim took his place on the fifty.

The drum major gave the signal to begin and Tim sounded the opening phrase of the fiddler's theme with a tone that was beautifully clear and confident. (It may have been a summer night under the lights in Bloomington, but it was springtime, sunshine and roses for me.) My heart suddenly bubbled its way back up to its normal place in my ribcage and everything was again right with the world. At the end of the Vanguard show I climbed down from my lonely perch in the end zone and found myself accosted by staff members exclaiming that Tim had been absolutely on fire during the performance.

I asked Tim immediately after the performance if the Tic Tac was of any help, and he said, with an exaggerated "uh-oh" expression on his face, that he had forgotten all about it, as he popped the Tic Tac into his mouth.

So far so good!

Chapter 47
1992 Drum Corps Perspective

1992 marked my fortieth year in drum corps. Over those forty years drum and bugle corps had changed immensely. They had evolved. East coast visionaries, the likes of Jim Donnelly, Bill Hayes, and Bobby Adair, propelled junior drum corps out of the age of military calls and flourishes played on open G bugles, and into the age of multi voiced, diatonic brass ensembles playing the music of Broadway, Sousa, and the concert stage.

By the mid fifties drum corps had reached a solid developmental plateau. They exhibited highly developed percussion lines, generally consisting of eight leg drums (four snare and four tenor), two bass drums, and two pairs of cymbals. As of 1956, hornlines numbered in the twenties and low thirties and were composed of assortments of soprano, small bell baritone, bass baritone, and French horn bugles. These were single valve bugles with tuning slides, which were not yet allowed in VFW competition for the purpose of playing chromatic (illegal) notes. But the days of sharps and flats in drum and bugle corps were not far off.

Colorguards in the mid fifties consisted of an American flag, with an honor guard comprised of a state flag, two or three service flags, and a pair of rifles or sabers. The American flag, complete with its honor guard, was a necessary requirement for participation in VFW and American Legion competitions.

Actually there were many requirements, restrictions, and regulations placed on drum corps in those early days. Every corps had to enter the field of competition over the starting line. This meant that every corps started with all of its personnel lined up in a straight line, forming a company front, on the left goal line. Each corps had to average a tempo of one hundred and thirty beats per minute throughout their show. Each corps was required to play a color presentation to honor the American flag. All shows were to be between thirteen and fifteen minutes in duration. All corps were required to leave the field of competition by exiting over the finish line located at the right goal line.

All of these rules and regulations served to establish a basic form for drum corps shows. Most drum corps would begin with a fanfare on the starting line and then move downfield with some good traveling music. At the end of the opening production there would be a brief percussion feature that might lead into a color presentation, which then typically led to a percussion feature, an into concert production, a standstill concert, an out of concert production, a short percussion feature, and a closing production complete with closing fanfare.

Since the opening production had to move from the left goal line (starting line) to center of the field, and the closing production required a lateral sweep to the right goal (finish line), the center portion of the show was performed in the center of the field. This middle portion would incorporate various backfield moves and full frontal presentations, such as the full corps company front into the stands with a rousing melody, which was always a big crowd favorite.

By the end of the sixties, hornlines had increased in size to fifty or more brass performers, and had added the contrabass, the mellophone and the flugelhorn to their growing arsenal of instruments. Percussion sections grew larger with as many as eight snare drums, four quad (tenor) drums, four tuned bass drums, tympani, and cymbals. But the biggest change in drum corps during the '60s was by far in the area of colorguard. Colorguards had increased dramatically in size by the end of the sixties and were now twirling their flags as well as spinning and tossing their rifles.

The 1970s brought sweeping changes for drum corps. By the end of the '70s, hornlines were numbering in the sixties, and had added the euphonium to their ensemble texture. Field percussion numbered into the twenties with ten snares, five quads, five tuned bass, and cymbals. But in addition, there was now a percussion pit, which was comprised of just about everything you could hit, bang, or bong. There were huge bass drums, gongs, tympani, xylophones, vibraphones, bells, chimes, marimbas, and more cymbals than you would care to hear struck at once. (The pit was located just ahead of the front sideline between the forty-yard lines.) Colorguards had grown bigger and better than ever with spinning flags, flying rifles, and flowered hoopdedos.

Tempo restrictions were gone. The starting line and finish line were gone. The color presentation requirement was gone. The show lengths were shortened. There were no more timing guns fired off at the end of shows to mar the sound of recordings. Show designers had a free hand to see what their designing minds could create.

The biggest change for me in the 1980s was the demise of the standstill concert. Instead of a two-minute standstill concert the trend went toward short "park and blow" sections during the show. I remember as a spectator, back in the day, the concert was my favorite part of the show because the brass performers would get a chance to really show their stuff.

Colorguards broke from the traditional military style uniforms in the '80s and donned costumes more appropriate to dance. The American flag was nowhere to be seen, unless used as a prop for a patriotic effect.

And the big change in percussion during the 1980s were those hard plastic top heads on the snare drums, which dramatically changed the characteristic sound of drum corps' field percussion ensemble. Snare drums had been equipped with plastic heads for years, but these heads were high tensioned and hard as concrete.

* * *

So at the 1992 World Championships held in Madison, Wisconsin, on August 15th, Edie and I sat in the stands and watched the top six corps in the world perform. To say the least, I was disappointed, except for the final corps, The Chicago Cavaliers: The Green Machine!

Before the Cavaliers performed that evening I had been wondering if maybe I was just burned out on drum corps. Not one of the corps had been able to capture or hold my interest. Edie was getting tired of my whining about the quality of the shows. Not one of the shows made any musical or visual sense to me. They didn't gather momentum or build to climaxes. One production followed another but without any meaningful ebb and flow. The end of one production did not hand the observer's imagination off to the beginning of the next production. There was no theatrical, emotional glue holding things together.

But the Cavaliers' show grabbed my attention immediately. They were captivating. It seemed as if the performers were all being controlled by the same mind. The opening visual production was mesmerizing. It was entertaining! It transported the observer from the mundane world of everyday existence to a well thought out and beautifully executed three-dimensional spectacle of audio-visual delight. That was all it took! I hadn't been burned out… I had been bored! Thank God for the Cavaliers in 1992.

* * *

Tim had a great performance with the Vanguard on finals night. It was a very emotional show. The corps truly wanted to show what they were capable of despite the chaos of the last few months. And that was exactly what they did. I would venture to say that the *Bottle Dance*, at the conclusion of the Vanguard show, generated the largest single ovation at Camp Randall Stadium that evening.

After the show, Gail Royer, the founding father of the Santa Clara Vanguard, conducted the Vanguard brass ensemble through his favorite piece, *Send in the Clowns*, for the very last time. Gail R. Royer passed away on June 17th, 1993.

Chapter 48
1993 Towards the Future

By the end of 1992 I had finally decided the direction I would take for the future of my professional life. I had always been interested in the reciprocal workings of the human mind and body. The mind body connection is the underlying theme of yoga and meditation. I had decided to practice the ancient art of bodywork, but not just bodywork. I wanted to incorporate bodywork into a holistic approach to promote and secure a healthy rapport between certain neurological aspects and physical attributes of injured individuals.

My hope was to use everything I had learned and experienced to help solve the problems facing professional musicians. To accomplish this goal I took courses in basic massage techniques and human physiology to become certified. Repetitive strain disorders and their destructive effects on peoples' lives had been the buzz topic during the early '90s. I studied everything I could get my hands on in relation to repetitive strain and musicians' performance disorders. In addition, I read extensively in the fields of clinical hypnotism, self-hypnotism, creative imagery, energy healing, autonomic nervous system health, and deep trance.

I was gearing up for a future that would captivate my interest, and I was hoping for some good fortune to come my way and afford me the break I would need to be successful.

* * *

In 1993 I had worked with only two drum corps. One was the Allegiance Elite in Alberta, and the other was the Skyriders, located just outside of Dallas, Texas. Both corps were in need of new musical repertoires. I asked John if he was interested in writing the shows and he jumped at the opportunity. So I purchased a Korg M1 and a computer interface for him to get started with, and John did the rest. That was the beginning of John's career as a marching music show designer.

Along with their music, John and Tim also spent time following in Edie's footsteps. They became bank tellers. John had started working at a small local bank in September of '91 and was saving up in preparation for his forthcoming marriage to Jackie Woodley in May of '93. Tim had just graduated from high school in June of '92, and after drum corps season, went to work for the Bank of America. Tim had decided not to march the '93 season and was saving up to buy a new Honda Civic.

* * *

During the '93 season I had the distinct pleasure of meeting and working with a wonderful young musician, teacher, and human being. His name is Paul Rennick. He was percussion caption head for the Skyriders drum and bugle corps at the time. Paul exhibited the same intense, single-minded focus that I had observed in Fred Sanford, Rick Odello, Dennis Delucia, and Mark Thurston. Paul was quiet, friendly, laid back, and easy to be with, but always intense. His offbeat brand of humor made the experience of working in the hot and humid Texas climate fun and memorable.

Paul Rennick went on to become one of the most sought-after percussion instructors in the drum corps activity, winning three of the last five Fred Sanford high percussion awards at the DCI World Championships.

* * *

In September of '93, my son John was offered a position on the Blue Devil brass staff. John accepted the offer and my son Tim held true to his often-stated intention to return to the Blue Devils for the '94 season. The Meehans were back with BD.

* * *

On June 25th of 1994 I went to my first ever California drum corps competition as a spectator. I was there to see my two wonderful boys do their thing. While walking along the track in front of the stands I heard my name being called out. I turned to see Dr. Frank Wilson waving frantically at me from the front row. I hadn't seen or spoken with the good doctor for quite some time, years in fact.

(Allow me to point out that if John and Tim had not returned to the Blue Devils, I would not have been at the Concord show that evening to meet up with Dr. Frank Wilson, and, I would therefore never have had the life changing conversation that ensued.)

Frank asked if I was still teaching, to which I replied that the torch had been passed on to the next generation, but that I had just recently completed course work in massage therapy. Frank's eyes grew wide and his eyebrows popped up like umbrellas as he said, "Really? Well then! You should come see me at Kaiser and I'll put you to work."

See what I mean? Intentionally envisioning all of those initial goals, thoughts, and images, had the effect of broadcasting my future hopes and dreams to the universe. The message had been sent out loud and clear, and Dr. Wilson must have received it five by five. And, since I had already done all the work necessary to be fully prepared for my opportunity when it serendipitously presented itself, I was able to answer Frank's statement with a question, "When do we start?" To which Frank replied, "How about next Wednesday at 3:00?

And that was that!

I floated a few feet off the ground for the rest of the evening.

* * *

My son Tim's demeanor that night was more intense than I could ever remember. Tim's main focus in 1994 was to become a leader in the Blue Devil hornline, and his experience and personality dictated that he would be most effective at being a leader by providing a first-rate example. He used his wealth of drum corps experience to help focus his fellow performers' intentions onto the here and now of great performance. But in addition, Tim's overriding intention was to win the DCI World Championship. After fourteen years of marching and playing his bugle, Tim wanted a DCI ring, and he was determined to succeed!

It was wonderful to see and hear Tim back on the field that evening. His solo was sizzling hot, and his individual presence on the field was superb. As Frankie Valli and the Four Seasons once sang so eloquently, "Oh what a night."

The Blue Devils went undefeated in 1994 and won the DCI World title with a score of 98.4. Tim had successfully followed his dream and finally obtained his DCI ring. His drum corps journey was complete. John, on the other hand, was just beginning his career as a Blue Devil brass instructor. He is presently in his seventeenth year on the Blue Devil staff and has been in complete charge of the brass caption for the last four years. During those four years the Blue Devils have won three out of the four world championships, and in 2010, the corps went undefeated for the entire season in brass, for the first time since 1988.

Chapter 49
That's My Story

So, that's my story, and I'm sticking to it!

I had no clue as to what I was getting myself into when the idea first came to me to write this memoir. It has now been three years, almost to the day, and I have successfully downloaded all the mental madness and stuffed it into my digital memory box. I remember keying in the very first page of the manuscript, observing how the mental images came to life upon the screen; scenes of my past were being etched into the fabric of history. It is still hard for me to believe that all those memories, thoughts, and creations were stored in my brain. They had always existed there but they had existed without form. Now I have given them form.

The process of delving into my past was tricky to deal with at first. I was essentially living two separate lives. I was living my life in the present and reliving my life of the past. I was writing my true-life story at the same time as I was seeing twenty-five people a week in my real life practice. The faded mental recollections of my past life were slowly infringing upon the focus of my life in the present. I would frequently find myself sucked down into the mired details of that which I was recalling for the memoir, while presently engaged in my ongoing work with clients. This was not a good thing. I stopped writing in order to figure out the "how to" of handling the situation copacetically.

I found it necessary to keep my mind focused on the positive progress of my past life, and not indulge myself in its negative aspects. It wasn't so much the memories that were causing problems, it was the emotions that were tied to those memories. I decided it was unfortunate that the "bad" stuff had happened in the first place but that no good was going to come from wallowing in the pallid memories of situations gone wrong. I had to stay positive in my recall of the past, which was not really a stretch for me since I have always been a proponent of the power of positive thinking.

The inspiration to write this memoir came to me as a result of my son John's work with the Blue Devils in 2007. John had finally been given the situational control he needed to craft his vision of a great drum corps brass ensemble, and by midseason of 2007 he was well on his way to doing that.

The fact that the DCI championships were being held on the west coast for the first time in history added fuel to the fire that was burning inside me to tell my story.

During finals week I had the opportunity to observe John as he took the Blue Devil hornline through their paces. It was a singular thrill that I will never forget. Here was my son, doing what I had done for so many years, fulfilling the dreams and expectations of the dedicated performers of the Blue Devil brass ensemble by creating a monster of a hornline that could thrill and excite the drum corps world. I felt inspired by the fact that it had finally gone full circle. This was a story that spanned sixty years of drum corps history and I wanted to tell it.

During the week of rehearsals that led up to finals, I was time and again heartened by the obvious respect shown by the staff toward the brass, percussion, and colorguard ensembles. The performers were given instruction in an intelligent, respectful, and honest way. Schedules were adhered to, and rehearsal periods were well designed and run in a way to sharpen performance without diminishing spirit. So in retrospect, I was seeing the results of the silent war I had waged all those years ago at my first Blue Devil rehearsal. Dignity and mutual human respect had finally won out.

Through John's organizational and leadership skills, the Blue Devil brass ensemble is once again being tuned with the same care and understanding that I had held to in the '80s. The corps is back to using the highest quality brass instruments available, and the performers are once again being equipped with matched sets of well-designed mouthpieces. And perhaps the best news of all is that John's prowess and creativity with my favorite adrenalin pumper, Space Music, knows no bounds. John has developed more hand signals than a major league batting coach.

Since 1978, the Blue Devils have won twelve DCI World Championships, always with a Meehan teaching brass.

Chapter 50
The Final Critique

Over the years, five basic performance qualities have been debated at drum corps conventions, symposiums, and critiques. They are: execution, esprit de corps, entertainment value, demand, and innovation.

In the early days of drum corps, execution was said to be the name of the game. No matter what a corps did, it had to be done cleanly. Depending on whether it was VFW or American Legion rules, execution counted for seventy to ninety percent of the total score. Precise execution was the basis upon which drum corps were judged.

Number two on the list of hotly debated items has been esprit de corps, which is defined as a shared spirit of comradeship, enthusiasm, and devotion to a cause among the members of a group, for example of a military unit. This reminds us that drum corps flourished from a military organization, and that means spit shined, sharp as a razor's edge, with a well-honed singular focus.

An important byproduct of esprit de corps is passion. Passionate people become energized in the face of problems. They get their kicks from performing beyond expectations. They inspire people to routinely do the impossible. Problems and setbacks are merely hurdles to be crossed with care. Passionate leaders are totally committed to excellence; nothing less will satisfy. The brass ring is what they seek and what they must have.

When drum corps performers become truly passionate about the quality of their individual performance, their personal potential for spirited execution rises to new levels. Heartfelt passion adds a whole new dimension to the art of performance. It adds sparkle without using lights or glitter.

Drum corps were originally valued and appreciated for their high intensity, precision performances, and as far as I am concerned that is still the hallmark of the finest drum corps performances of all time. The truth is that without clean, spirited execution, one cannot fully appreciate a show's entertainment value, demand, or innovation. Clean, crisp performance is what catapulted drum and bugle corps into the American spotlight in the first place, and it is what will help to propel the activity well into the future.

Mr. Jones used to say that drum corps was the art of the possible. The closer one comes to designing the impossible, the lower the probability of scoring well in execution, and execution is the name of the game. Mr. Jones believed whole-heartedly in pushing his performers right to their limit, but he knew where to draw the line. He knew to keep a balance between that which he could imagine and that which he could accomplish, given the high level of performance he demanded from the Troopers.

I think the perfect example of a highly spirited, crisply executed drum corps show was the performance the Anaheim Kingsmen gave the night they won the first ever DCI World Championship in 1972. It sparkled with precision and clarity. The man who spearheaded the corps' attitude and work ethic had been a military man, a United States Marine. Spit shined and clean as a whistle, mentally tough and singularly focused on the objective… Grrrrr!

* * *

Entertainment value is a tough concept to wrap your head around. As Howard Dietz once said, it's the clown with his pants falling down or the dance that's a dream of romance or the scene where the villain is mean. That's entertainment! It might be a fight like you see on the screen, or a swain getting slain for the love of a queen, or some great Shakespearean scene where a ghost and a prince meet, and everyone ends in mincemeat. The guy, who was waving the flag that began, with the mystical hand, hip hooray! The American way! The world is a stage; the stage is a world of entertainment!

Entertainment takes us to a different world. It feeds our need for fantasy and provides an escape from real life. A truly fine drum corps performance can transpose observers to a world of fantasy, grabbing at their attention, until they become part of the show's alternative reality. That's entertainment!

* * *

During the early seventies, the drum corps community raised the difficulty/demand banner on high. Difficulty and demand: difficulty meaning more intricately involved, requiring a higher degree of technique, or presenting a greater likelihood of error. While demand refers to the physical and mental demands placed on the performer such as stamina, endurance, multiple responsibility requirements, and range of intensities.

The truth is, putting a modern drum and bugle corps on the field is difficult and demanding enough. But difficulty and demand credit is only given for that which is over the top. In many cases, evaluating difficulty and demand is like trying to compare the attributes of oranges, apples, birds, and fish: very difficult to evaluate fairly or accurately. But difficulty and demand are important aspects of performance, and need to be taken into consideration when searching for the ultimate drum corps.

* * *

The drum corps activity has been blessed with many fine innovators over the years whose dreams and hard work have advanced our activity greatly. Like consummate artists contributing to a universal palette of ideas, they have created a repertoire of proven possibilities for future designers, writers, and arrangers to draw from.

To my way of thinking, however, a really well designed, beautifully executed show is an innovation in and of itself. I have personally experienced many wonderful drum corps performances, some innovative and some classic, but all were beautifully designed and inspiringly executed.

The big innovation going on in drum corps today is in the realm of show design, and the winningest drum corps in history is leading the way. The Blue Devils' creative team and staff have produced shows over the last four years that have explored the boundaries and possibilities of performance with an unfettered, no holds barred approach.

Visual design innovators Jim Jones, Steve Brubaker, Pete Emmons, and George Zingali were highly musical in the way they applied their own special creations of linear and curvilinear design to the musical show. Their true genius was in their ability to marry music to motion. When visual designers support and complement the energy, feel, mood, and emotion of the music, performers are able to more naturally interpret the mood of their show's many complex responsibilities. It just has to feel right!

When a show is masterfully interpreted through the art of creative visual design, the audience, on some level, gets it. They become mesmerized by the unity, power, and spontaneity of it all. And when this visual treat is added to a musical score dripping with style, sweetness, driving rhythms, and grandiose spectacle, and is performed in a precise, spirited fashion, you have the makings of a DCI champion.

Chapter 51
Final Thoughts

I have observed and identified five key attributes for personal success. They are: proper preparation, postural awareness, mental clarity, strong intention, and consistent application.

Always be prepared!

Being prepared is all about being at your best. It is about being well rested, and at the same time mentally, physically, and emotionally healthy. Balanced, on track, in the moment, in the groove, ready to tackle anything that comes along, mentally, physically, and emotionally one hundred percent ready, present, and accounted for.

Being prepared also means knowing your subject matter well! Seek out experiential information. Create a strong foundation of knowledge and understanding about what it is you intend to do. Plan ahead, but be prepared to improvise as you go. Form a mental image of that which you wish to see happen. Build your future first in your mind, and then create it in reality, using your hands, heart, and talents. Always keep your eye on the target. Never become discouraged.

Balance your posture!

Your posture affects your attitude, and your attitude affects your future success as an individual. Balanced posture expresses willful control over the most powerful force on earth: gravity. Balanced posture defies and defeats the long-term destructive effects of gravity. A powerful and buoyant posture breeds self-confidence. It encourages you to take a chance: to actively seek after what you truly want out of life. When your posture is correct, your muscles, organs, joints, and bones are held in a state of proper alignment. There is no strain. A physical state of balance and ease exits within you.

While a state of balance obviously refers to good posture, it also relates to your psychological profile. Correct posture is directly related to an ideal state of mind: being off balance physically disturbs your mind in subtle ways. Impeccable balance exudes the benefits of body/mind discipline. It engenders a sense of power. Movement becomes free and easy. It's as if you've just hit a home run. You are sure of yourself, poised, and secure. You have the ability to handle adverse situations with zeal. You are at your best when you are relaxed, focused, and balanced.

Clear your mind!

Your mind is potentially at its most powerful when it is at rest: all of its abilities online and ready to go, calmly awaiting your every whim: calm, clear, collected and aware. Just imagine, the sum total of your mind's considerable powers, all gathered together, ready to be focused and unleashed on some unsuspecting project.

A clear mind is arguably the highest achievement one could possibly wish to accomplish. A clear mind allows you to be comfortable within your own skin. A clear mind is the definition of a mind at peace... and being at peace, at rest, free of worrisome thought, stimulates the parasympathetic branch of the autonomic nervous system.

The parasympathetic system of nerves is concerned with the healing, nourishment, and regeneration of the body. It is anabolic, meaning that its primary job is to rebuild the body. Its nerves stimulate digestion, energize the immune system, and operate the eliminative organs. The parasympathetic nervous system, when activated by rest, relaxation and happy thoughts, is essential for balanced living. Instituting a healthy parasympathetic state, and staying there for as much time as possible, helps to heal all physical and emotional maladies.

Develop a strong, clear intention!

People who foster strong, clear intentions accomplish many wonderful things. A strong, clear intention constitutes a dedication to action. It is a fervent desire to see something through to conclusion. All intentions are not necessarily strong, all intentions are not necessarily clear, but any intention can be improved upon. To improve upon an intention focus more clearly on exactly what it is you are attempting to accomplish. Then clear your mind of all other cares and go for the gold. A strong clear intention is like an arrow being shot from a bow, aimed at a big bulls-eye. Straight and true the arrow flies, without hesitation, without distraction, without question, without faltering, constantly vectoring in on the target of choice.

A clear intention sets specific direction. It wields power, instigates action, puts the wind in your sails, and gives your ideas traction! It is powered by an energy source emanating from deep within. It entails planning, imagination, and sometimes, hard work. An example of clear intention would be the singular intention to make music when picking up a musical instrument, and to maintain that focus while performing.

Of the infinite number of possible human intentions the most basic of all is to survive: to stay alive, and live to see another day. Constant, well-focused awareness is absolutely necessary, and key, to surviving in a hostile environment. The same high degree of focus and awareness that was afforded our cave dwelling ancestors as they battled each day to stay alive, is available to anyone who is willing to stir the internal hornet's nest of driving desires. In order to fully activate your age-old quickened awareness, and to reignite the instinctive intention to survive, accomplish, and evolve, you must commit yourself fully and consistently to your dreams, goals, and ambitions... Pretty intense, huh?

Be consistent!

Be consistent, steady, reliable, dependable, unswerving, and always remember that all great ideas demand consistent application!

People who are consistent just keep plugging away. Slow and steady wins the race. All great journeys start with a single step. When you act in a consistent manner, you create the day-to-day glue that connects together everything you do. When you knowingly implement the four personal attributes of proper preparation, postural awareness, mental clarity, and clear intention, on a consistent day-to-day basis, you discover that your expectations and hopes for the future turn positive and powerful, naturally. No matter the situation, no matter the obstacle, no matter the odds, you can be ready, willing and able to take on the challenges that come your way and strategically see them through to The End.

Oh how Zen like…

* * *

We are entities of energy floating in a celestial ocean of energy in motion. We are all connected through this unlimited ocean, which undulates and stirs with the movement of the stars, sending mighty currents across the universe to Mars. We are energy in motion throughout a vast celestial ocean, surging with the origins of creation. Through canyons and cities, over oceans and land, the power of the cosmos is there in your hand. Avail yourself of these energy streams, use the force to build your dreams.

Photo by Ashley Meehan

Birthday buddies Jack and granddaughter Katelyn born
at the same time on the same day, fifty eight years apart.

Jack and his lovely wife Edie live in Martinez, California
within walking distance of their children and grandchildren.

Come visit us on the web at JackMeehan.com

Made in the USA
San Bernardino, CA
07 January 2013